Contents

To the student

How will this book help me?

This book will help you to write better paragraphs in English. 'Better writing' means writing that is:

- more accurate   • easier to read   • appropriate to the reader   • more interesting

Why is it important to be accurate?

For most kinds of writing it is important to make sure that spelling, punctuation and grammar are correct. If you make mistakes in speech it doesn't usually matter much, as long as people understand your meaning. But when you write, people expect much more accuracy, especially if you are writing as part of your job (letters, reports, etc.) or as part of your studies (essays, examinations, etc.)

What does 'easier to read' mean?

This means that the writing is more fluent. The sentences are not too short and not too long. They link together neatly so that the meaning in one sentence is carried into the next, and so on. As a result, it is easy for the reader to 'get the message' – to find out what you want to say.

How do I know if my writing is 'appropriate'?

Find out about different writing styles. The way you write to a friend is not the same way that you write to a new boss or the head of a college. Learn about formal and informal language. When you write, imagine the reader. What does he or she expect from your writing? That will also make your writing more interesting!

How can I make my writing 'better'?

1. Go through *Better Writing* and complete all the units. In each unit, the first section ('Looking at text') asks you to look at material other people have written. It picks out language points which are important to understand if you are going to write well, and it gives you exercises to practise that language. The remaining sections of each unit focus on other things which will help you write better. Each unit contains a section on sentence building, ways of joining short sentences together, improving the way you put sentences together to make paragraphs, punctuation, checking (or 'editing') what you have written, and building your vocabulary.

2. Reading helps writing, so read as much as you can in English. Read anything that is interesting and not too difficult for you. Try graded readers, newspapers, magazine articles, information on the Internet and even advertisements or airline brochures.

3. When you read, be aware of different styles of English.

Good luck!

Describing things

Looking at text

1 **Maria, Salah, Yoko and Tony are writing to friends. Read the four paragraphs and match these people with the pictures. Write their names below the pictures.**

_____ _____ _____ _____

Maria is writing a letter to a friend in Singapore.

I've got a new mobile phone. It's quite light and it's small, so it's easy to carry in my pocket. It weighs 300g and it's only 15cm long. It has a black leather case to protect it. I love it! I can keep in touch with my family and friends all the time. It's got large, luminous numbers, so I can read them easily in the dark. I use the phone when I go shopping. I also take it with me to the college, although I have to switch it off in class!

Salah is sending an e-mail message to a friend in Japan.

My brother bought a jeep a couple of weeks ago. It's in excellent condition, although it's second-hand. I think it's about four years old. It's a Yakono Land Cruiser with air-conditioning and power steering. It's quite fast, and of course it's got four-wheel drive. My brother uses the car when he goes camping in the desert. The air-conditioning is fantastic. It's also got a roof-rack on the top, which is very useful for luggage and water containers. There's also a spare tyre on the back. I hope he'll let me borrow the jeep sometimes!

Yoko is also sending an e-mail – to Habiba, a friend in Tehran.

> I've got a new watch. My cousin gave it to me last week. It's quite attractive, but it's very unusual! It's made of plastic and the style is very modern. I think it's French. The face of the watch is square in shape and it's red with long white hands. It's a very big watch, and the face measures nearly 5cm across! There are no numbers on the face, which is strange. It hasn't got the date on it either. The strap is also red and is made of plastic. I think I like the watch, but I'm not sure!

Tony is writing to a friend in Sweden.

> I've got some good news. My brother and I have got a boat! We bought it last week. It's not new, but it's in good condition. I think it looks beautiful sailing through the waves. It's made of fibreglass, so it's very light. There's a mast in the middle with a sail. The boat is about 5m long and the mast is 4m high. It's not very fast, but we're very happy with it. The boat is white and the sail is dark blue. Its name is 'Sunbird'. It's quite a good name, don't you think?

2 **Read through the paragraphs again.**

a. Underline all the verbs that belong with *got*. For example, in line 1 of Maria's letter, *I've got* should be underlined.

b. What do you think *'s* and *'ve* mean?

 's = _____   've = _____

3 ## Language: *have got/has got*

I **have** got ...	She **has** got ...	We **have** got ...
You **have** got ...	It **has** got ...	You **have** got ...
He **has** got ...		They **have** got ...

Look at these sentences:
I **have got** a new watch. (I**'ve got** a new watch.)
It **has got** four-wheel drive. (It**'s got** four-wheel drive.)
We **have go**t a boat. (We**'ve got** a boat.)

We can also say:
I **have** a new watch.
It **has** four-wheel drive.
We **have** a boat.
Note: This is more common in North American English.

Write sentences about Salah's brother, Yoko, Tony and his brother, the jeep and the boat. Use *has/have (got)*.

Example: *Maria has got a new mobile phone.*

a. *Salah's brother* _____

b. _____

c. _____

d. _____

e. _____

4 **Language:** dimensions

Read these sentences:
The table is 2.3m **long**.
The table is 2.3m in **length**.
The **length** of the table is 2.3m.

Complete the table below.

ADJECTIVE	NOUN
long	*length*
wide	
high	
thick	

5 **Read this paragraph about Kuwait Towers and answer the questions on page 4.**

When visitors come to Kuwait, they should take a trip to Kuwait Towers. It is a beautiful and very famous monument situated on the coast road. It consists of three tall, thin towers, which are white in colour. It also has three blue spheres. The towers are wide at the base, but at the top they come to a point. They look like three space rockets pointing to the stars. The towers are not all the same size. The tallest is 187m high and has two spheres. There is a small sphere near the top and a large sphere near the middle. The next-tallest tower is 147m in height with one sphere. The third tower, the smallest, has not got any spheres. Inside the small sphere on the tallest tower there is a viewing area and a restaurant. When you go up in the lift, you can see the whole of Kuwait. It is a wonderful view. The towers and the spheres are used for storing water.

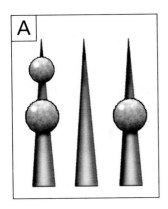 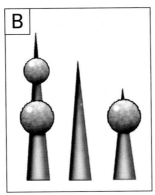 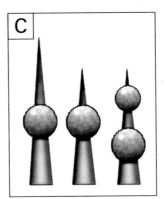 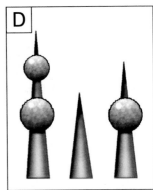

a. Look at the four drawings above. Which drawing shows Kuwait Towers? ____

Now complete these sentences:

b. The monument _____ three towers and three spheres.

c. The towers _____ in colour and the spheres _____ .

d. One sphere _____ large and the other _____ .

e. The towers and spheres _____ storing water.

Sentence building

6 **Put these sentences into the table below. Put the words in the correct order first.**

a. the back / engine / got / has / boat / a small / at / our

b. has / two / the sides / at / CD player / speakers / my / got

c. got / the front / have / at / shirts / two pockets / these

What?	Verb (have/has got)	What?	Where?	.
The jeep	has got	a roof-rack	on the top	.

7 **Look at the pictures on page 5. Make a sentence in your notebook about each picture. Follow this pattern:**

What?	Verb (have/has got)	What?	Where?	.

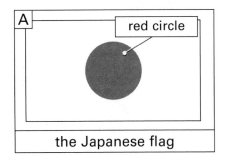

the Japanese flag

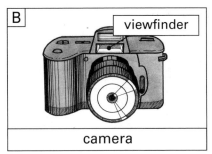

camera

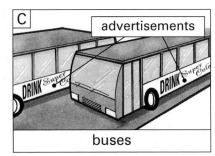

buses

8 **We can also describe things using *there*.**

There	Verb *(be)*	What?	Where?	.
There	*is*	*a roof-rack*	*on top of the jeep*	.

Rewrite the sentences about the three pictures using *there*. Put them in the table above.

9 **Language: *made of/used for***

Look at these sentences. Underline the verbs.

This shirt is made of cotton.

These boats are made of fibreglass.

The tower is used for storing water.

The spheres are used for storing water.

These kinds of verb consist of two parts:

to be
(is, are, was, etc.)

+

the past participle form
(made, used, built, etc.)

Now complete these sentences using these materials:

> metal   rubber   plastic   paper

a. *A credit card* _____

b. *A knife* _____

c. *Envelopes* _____

d. *Tyres* _____

What are the above things used for? Choose from the list and write a sentence about each in your notebook.

> sending letters   cutting things
> covering wheels   paying for goods and services

Joining ideas

 Language: *with*

Look at these sentences:	The watch is red. It has got white hands and a red strap.

We can join them using **with**.

First part of the sentence	*with*	What?
The watch is red	with	white hands and a red strap.

Now match these sentences. Use *with* to join the sentences.

The jeep is new.	It has large, luminous numbers.
The watch is oval.	It has tinted windows and power steering.
The phone is small.	It has a white mast and a red sail.
The boat is green.	It has silver hands and a gold strap.

a. *The jeep is new with* _____

b. _____

c. _____

d. _____

11 **Write a sentence about each of these things in your notebook. Use *with*.**

(My watch   Our house/flat/apartment   The classroom)

When clauses

12 **Look at the sentence in the table below. Then look at Maria's and Salah's paragraphs in Exercise 1 on page 1. Find two sentences which have *when* clauses and write them in the table below.**

Who?	Verb	What?	When?	.
We	use	the boat	when we go fishing	.

Underline the verbs in the *when* clauses. For example, *when we go fishing.*

13 **Add *when* clauses to these sentences. Write the sentences on the lines below.**

a. I usually take a camera with me.

b. My brother carries water on the roof-rack.

c. Mario never uses his mobile phone.

d. Yoko uses her computer.

First part of the sentence	*When* clause
I always wear my new watch	when I go to the university.

a. _____

b. _____

c. _____

d. _____

Check your sentences. Underline the verbs in the *when* clauses.

14 **Remember that it is also possible to begin a sentence with the *when* clause.**

Example: *When it rains in Beijing, ...*

Find two sentences beginning with *when* clauses in the paragraph about Kuwait Towers on page 3. Write them in the table below.

When clause	Last part of the sentence
When I go to the university,	*I always wear my new watch.*

Punctuation

15 **Language: contraction**

Look:

It's got ... = It **has** got ... BUT   It's very big. = It **is** very big. / It's made ... = It **is** made ...

7

Add punctuation and capital letters to this paragraph.

its got a memory but it hasn't got a brain it's rectangular in shape and quite thin it looks like a briefcase and is about the same size it's very easy to carry as it is made mostly of plastic and only weighs about 5kg when you open the lid you find a screen and a keyboard inside people use these machines when they are travelling what is it.

How many sentences are there? _____   What is it? It's a _____ .

Better paragraphs

16 **Look at paragraph A and paragraph B and answer these questions.**

a. How many sentences are there in paragraphs A and B? A _____ B _____

b. Underline things in paragraph B that are different from paragraph A. The first has been done for you.

c. Which paragraph do you think is better? _____ Why?

A I have got a new watch. The new watch was a present from my sister. Her name is Sarah. My sister is always very kind to me. The watch is oval in shape. It has a white face. The strap is black. The watch is waterproof. I go to the beach at weekends. I wear the watch then.

B I have got a new watch. It was a present from my sister, Sarah. She is always very kind to me. The watch is oval in shape with a white face and a black strap. The watch is waterproof and so I wear it when I go to the beach at weekends.

17 **Complete this paragraph describing a car. Use the words below.**

there   when   when   also   got   it   it   so   and   with

I'm thinking of selling my car, which is about six years old. It's a Gazelle, (a)_____ it's in quite good condition. The colour is grey (b)_____ dark blue stripes along the sides. (c)_____'s got a sun-roof and electric windows. I like to open the sun-roof (d)_____ the weather is not too hot. The engine is 2 litres, which is average size. Inside the car everything is black. (e)_____ is a CD player and very good air-conditioning. The seats are made of real leather and (f)_____ they are very comfortable. It's (g)_____ four new tyres and the spare tyre is (h) _____ in excellent condition. I hope to get about $4,000 for the car, (i)_____ I decide to sell (j)_____ .

18 **Complete this paragraph. Use the information in the picture to help you.**

A friend gave me a very beautiful and unusual present last week. It's a model of a (a)_____ and rider and is (b)_____ of iron. The base is (c)_____ in shape and measures about 40cm (d)_____ and 25cm (e)_____. The (f)_____ of the base is 5cm. The (g)_____ of the model is about 50cm. It's very heavy and (h)_____ more than 10kg. (i)_____'s a man on the horse. He's (j)_____ a sword in one hand and a (k)_____ in the other.

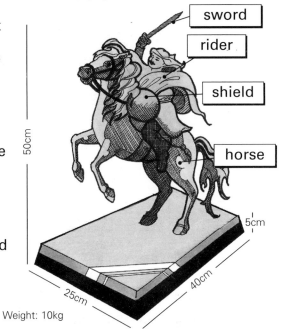

Weight: 10kg

Free writing

19 **Choose one of these watches. Write a paragraph about it in your notebook. Use Maria's paragraph on page 1 as an example.**

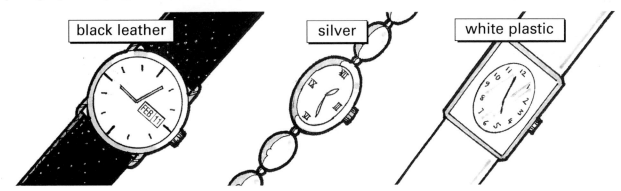

Show your paragraph to a partner. Ask him or her to say which watch you are describing.

20 **Look at this drawing of a boat. Write a paragraph in your notebook describing the boat.**

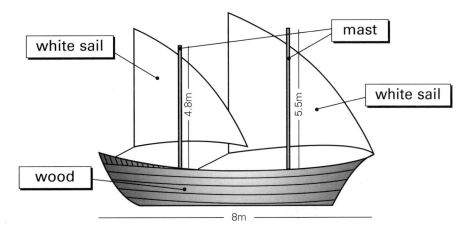

21 Look at the information in the table. It describes a new car. Write a paragraph about the new car for the readers of an automobile magazine. Use your notebook.

Model	Gazelle
Size	5 seater
Engine size	2.5 litres
Maximum speed	160kph
Air-conditioning	✓
Power steering	✓
Made in	Korea
Price	D 12,000
Extras	2 years' free service

22 Think about a monument in the country where you live. Write a paragraph in your notebook describing it. What does it consist of? How big is it? What is it made of? What does it look like? Is it used for anything?

Use this checklist to edit your writing in Exercises 19–22.

CHECKLIST	Exercise			
	19	20	21	22
How many sentences are there?				
How many full stops (.) are there?				
Does every sentence begin with a capital letter?				
Does every sentence have a verb?				
Have you checked your spelling?				
Can you make your writing **better**?				

Editing

23 Check the spelling, punctuation and grammar in this puzzle. There are ten mistakes.

It is got four legs, but it can't walk It has rectangular in shape and there is a leg at each corner. It measure about a metre in haight. the top is 1.8m long and 70cm waide and has a thickness of 4cm. Ours is made for wood, but sometimes they are made of plastic or glas. In our house we keep it in the dining Room.

What is it?   It's a _____.

24 There are no mistakes in this paragraph, but how can you make it better? Rewrite the paragraph in your notebook. These words will help you:

> he   it   with   and so   when

My friend Yi has got a new radio. Yi bought the radio a few days ago. The radio is black. The radio has a red handle. Yi likes the radio very much. The radio is very light. Yi can take the radio everywhere. He has a shower. He takes the radio with him.

Vocabulary building

Describing size

25 Put these words and phrases in order. Start with the smallest.

> quite big   very big   not very big   big

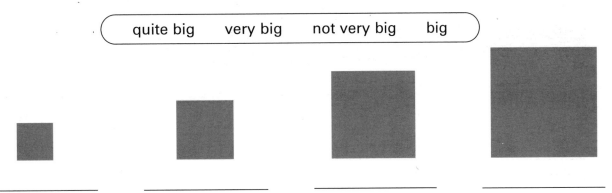

_____   _____   _____   _____

Use the words and phrases above to write sentences in your notebook about towns and cities you know.

Describing colours

26
Language: colours

| Look: | It's **black**. | The colour is **black**. | It's **black** in colour. |

Complete the colours in the list.

a. The sky at night is b_____.

b. The walls are w_____ in colour.

c. The sea is a bright b_____.

d. The colour of the sky that evening was r_____.

e. What a beautiful y_____ dress!

f. If you mix c) and e) you get g_____.

g. If you mix b) and d) you get p_____.

11

Describing materials

 What materials do you know? Add to this list.

It's made of ...

cotton   silk   metal   plastic   wood   gold   _____   _____

Now write a sentence for each in your notebook.

Example: *This shirt is made of cotton.*

Describing shape

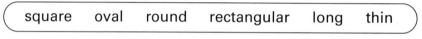

Language: shape

Look:

It's **square**.   It's **square** in shape.   It's shape is **square**.

Now match these pictures with the adjectives in the list.

square   oval   round   rectangular   long   thin

_____   _____   _____

_____

Describing condition

 Put these words in order in the list below.

quite good   very good   not very good   good

It's in *bad*_____ condition.   It's in _____ condition.

It's in _____ condition.   It's in _____ condition.

It's in _____ condition.   It's in *excellent*____ condition.

30 **Use these clues to complete the crossword below. Most of the words are in this unit.**

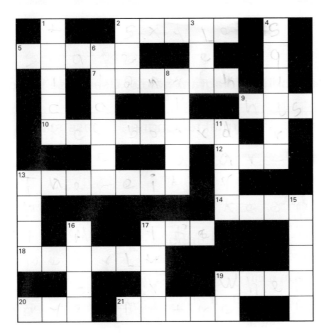

ACROSS

2. This statue is very modern in ___. (5 letters)
5. The ___ of the sail is triangular. (5)
7. The ___ of our boat is about 4m. (6)
9. My watch ___ got a round face. (3)
10. A computer has a screen and a ___. (8)
12. There ___ two water containers on the roof of the jeep. (3)
13. In the middle of the Japanese flag ___ ___ a red circle. (5,2)
14. With a mobile phone it's easy to ___ in touch with people. (4)
17. I have a new watch. My brother gave ___ watch to me last week. (3)
18. The population of Egypt is 58.6 million – that's ___ 60 million. (6)
19. I take my laptop computer with me ___ I go on a trip. (4)
20. You use your ___s to see. (3)
21. There are 100cm in one ___. (5)

DOWN

1. This carpet is very ___. It measures 3cm. (5 letters)
2. I'll give William the message when I ___ him. (3)
3. Will you ___ me borrow your boat for an hour? (3)
4. This room is ___ in shape. It measures 5.5m by 5.5m. (6)
6. I bought a new CD ___ last week. (6)
8. The boat is very light. It is made of fibre___. (5)
11. At night it is ___. (4)
13. The opposite of 1 Down. (4)
15. A mobile ___ is very useful when you are away from home. (5)
16. Is that necklace ___ of gold? (4)
17. It's important to carry a spare ___ when you drive in the desert. (4)
19. My friend and I have bought a new jeep. ___ are very happy with it. (2)

Describing how something works

Looking at text

1 **Read about mobile phones, then label the diagram below. Use these words:**

telephone exchange   normal telephone   base station

A mobile phone

A mobile phone, or cellular phone, is a very useful appliance. You can use it anywhere – at home, at college, in the street or in a car (but not when you are driving!) When you make a call to a friend, a signal <u>is sent</u> by your phone and collected by a base station. This is a special aerial which is situated on the top of tall buildings or hills. There are many of these aerials throughout a country or region, and they form a network of 'cells' which covers the whole area. The signal from your phone is then transferred to a cellphone exchange. If your friend has got an ordinary telephone, the signal is then passed to a normal telephone exchange. From there the signal is sent to their telephone and your friend receives your call. It's easy!

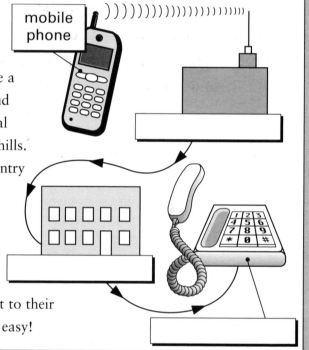

mobile phone

2 **Language:** passive verbs

Look at sentences a) and b). Underline the verbs.

a) The phone sends a signal.	b) A signal is sent by the phone.

The verb in sentence b) is a **passive verb**. We often use passive verbs when we explain how something (like a mobile phone) works.

a passive verb = *to be* + the past participle form

to be = *is/are/was/were/must be/can be*, etc.

past participle = (regular) *received/transmitted*, etc.
                  (irregular) *sent/made/built*, etc.

Now complete the tables.

What?	Verb	What?
a. *The phone*		

What?	Passive verb	By what?
b.		*by the phone.*

3 **Read the paragraph about mobile phones again.**

a. Underline all the passive verbs. The first one (*is sent*) has already been done for you.

b. There is one *when* clause. Underline it.

c. There is also one clause beginning with *if*. Underline it.

d. Find *it* in line 2, *This* in line 6 and *there* in line 14. *It* here means *a mobile phone*. What are the meanings of the other two words?

This = _____   there = _____

4 **Read this paragraph about answering machines. Who records the messages?**

a. The outgoing message is recorded by _____.

b. The incoming message is recorded by _____.

AN ANSWERING MACHINE

We've got a new answering machine at home. It's very useful and it's easy to use. First of all, someone living in the house has to record a message on the machine. This <u>is called</u> the 'outgoing' message. Usually people say something like – 'Hello. This is Athens 987 6543. We're not at home at the moment. Please leave a message after the "bleep".' When you go out, switch the machine on. When callers phone you, they hear your message and they can then leave a message for you if they want. The 'incoming' messages are recorded onto your machine and stored. A display on the machine shows you how many messages you've got. When you get home, press the 'play' button and listen to your messages. The messages can be played again and again if necessary.

5 **Read the paragraph again.**

a. The passive verb *is called* is underlined. Underline all the other passive verbs in the paragraph.

b. There are three *when* clauses. Underline them.

c. Write an outgoing message for your phone. _____

_____

_____

6 ## Language: instructions

When we describe how something works we often give instructions. Look at these instructions and underline the verbs.

a. Switch on the answering machine when you go out.

b. Leave a message after the 'bleep'.

c. Press the 'play' button when you want to listen to your messages.

We use the infinitive form of the verb (without *to*) for instructions:

to switch on ... = **switch on ...**

Now write sentences a), b) and c) in the table below.

Verb	What?	When?
a.		
b.		
c.		

 7 **Read this paragraph about a juice extractor.**

The Pulpex Juice Extractor

Congratulations on choosing a Pulpex Juice Extractor! It is made of extra-strong plastic and is guaranteed for five years. A juice extractor is a healthy way of enjoying fruit and vegetables. This is how it works. First of all, the fruit and vegetables must be washed carefully under a tap. They should then be peeled (if necessary) and cut into small pieces. The machine is then switched on and the pieces are pushed carefully into the feed tube using the pusher (do **not** use your fingers!). As the machine spins around, juice is separated from the pulp in the pulp collector. The juice flows from the outlet in the pulp collector and is collected in the juice jug.

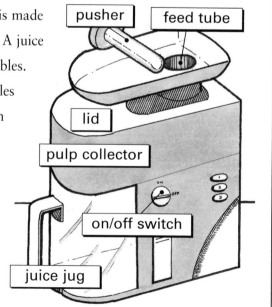

pusher · feed tube · lid · pulp collector · on/off switch · juice jug

a. Underline the passive verbs.

b. Put the diagrams below in order by numbering them 1–6.

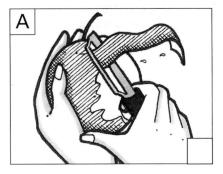

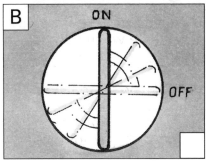

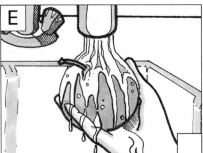

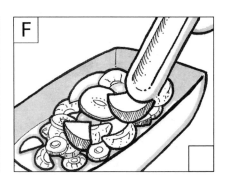

c. Now write these past participles under the pictures:

> collected   washed   cut   switched on   pushed   peeled

8 **Read the last part of the text about the juice extractor.**

> If the pulp container becomes full, switch off the machine, remove the lid and clean out the container. Finally, in order to enjoy a delicious drink full of vitamins, remove the jug and pour the juice into glasses.

a. Underline the *if* clause.

b. Underline the phrase beginning with *in order to*.

c. Find four instructions and write them in your notebook. Follow this pattern:

Verb	What?
Switch off	the machine.

Sentence building

9 These sentences all have passive verbs. First put the words in the correct order and then write them in the table below. They describe how a portable CD player works.

a. compartment / inserted / R6 batteries / into / are / two / the

b. placed / the / CD tray / a / is / on / CD

c. closed / must / lid / firmly / the / be

d. the front of / the CD player / headphones / are fitted / the / to

e. are / over / the / the / ears / placed / headphones

f. pressed / the / is / button / 'play'

g. can / as required / the / be / volume / adjusted

What?	Passive verb	How? Where? When?	.
The lid	*is removed*	*from the battery compartment*	.
a.			
b.			
c.			
d.			
e.			
f.			
g.			

10 Rewrite the sentences in the table above as instructions. Use your notebook.

Example: *Remove the lid from the battery compartment.*

11 Look at these pictures. Write a sentence in your notebook about each picture using a passive verb. Use the verb in brackets.

Example:
(cool)   *Food is cooled in a refrigerator.*

  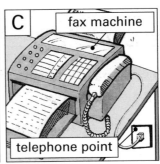 

a. (link) _____

_____

b. (plant) _____

_____

c. (connect) _____

_____

d. (open) _____

_____

Joining ideas

 Language: joining passive sentences

Look:

The fruit and vegetables are washed. They are cleaned.
The fruit and vegetables are washed and cleaned.

The machine is switched off. The pulp is removed.
The machine is switched off and the pulp removed.

Now join these sentences in the same way. Use your notebook.

a. The vegetables are peeled. They are cut into small pieces.

b. The signal is sent to an aerial. It is then transmitted to a telephone exchange.

c. The phone is made of plastic. The case is made of leather.

d. The outgoing message is recorded. The machine is switched on.

13 | **Language:** *as* clauses (time)

To show that two things are happening at the same time we can use an *as clause* of time.

When (*As* ...)	Last part of the sentence	.
As you speak into the answering machine,	*your voice is recorded*	.

Find another example of a sentence with an *as* clause in the paragraph about the juice extractor on page 16. Write it in the table above.

14 | **Language:** *if* clauses

An *if clause* tells us about a possibility.

If ...	Last part of the sentence	.
If you want to listen to the message,	*press the 'play' button*	.

Note: *If* and *as clauses* can be added to the beginning or the end of a sentence.

Look at the paragraph about mobile phones on page 14. Find an example of a sentence with an *if* clause. Write it in the table above.

15 Add clauses to these sentences. Remember that the clause must contain a verb.

a. As customers _____, they are filmed by video cameras.

b. Please remember to lock the door if you _____.

c. If passengers _____, they should go to the Lufthansa offices.

d. As passengers _____, they must show their tickets.

e. If you _____, you should see a doctor.

16 | **Language:** *in order to* ...

We use *in order to* **+ verb** (or just *to* + verb) to tell us **what** something is **for**:

In order to open the package, cut the corner with a knife.

Match these parts of sentences. Then write the sentences in the table below.

In order to make a phone call,   ... the amount of light must be measured.

To clean pulp from the extractor,   ... speak into the microphone.

In order to record the outgoing message,   ... the required number is keyed in.

To take good photographs,   ... the lid must be removed.

What for? (*In order to ...*)	Last part of the sentence	.
In order to start the machine,	*turn the control to number 1 or 2*	.
To clean the machine,	*the power must be switched off*	.

Punctuation

Apostrophes

 17 What is the difference between these sentences?

a. The student's books are on the desk.   b. The students' books are on the desk.

What is the difference between these sentences? Write them out in full.

c. The secretary's ill. _____

d. The secretary's got a fever. _____

18 Add apostrophes where they are needed. Some sentences do not need any changes.

a. The dogs got some bad cuts on its leg.

b. Im afraid the radios broken.

c. The girls are studying Physics and Economics.

d. Its situated at the top of a hill.

e. Theres a flag at the top of the building.

f. Messages are sent by computers.

g. The machines switched off at the moment.

h. Five teachers have their desks in this room. Its called the teachers room.

Clauses

 Find the clauses in these sentences. Add a comma if one is needed.

a. If the caller is in an underground car park it may be impossible to use the mobile phone.

b. When the tape is full no further messages can be recorded on the answering machine.

c. In order to avoid damage to the machine stones must be removed from fruit.

d. Contact your local dealer if you have problems with your new television.

e. As the door closes the light inside the refrigerator goes off.

f. In order to keep a compact disc in good condition it should be kept in its cover.

g. When someone leaves a message on the answering machine a number appears on the display panel.

h. The juice is separated from the pulp as the fruit is pushed into the feed tube.

Better paragraphs

 Read this paragraph about a hair drier.

The Superdry hair drier is easy to use and very light in weight. It comes in an attractive black canvas case. The drier has a very powerful motor which draws air into the machine and forces it out through a specially designed nozzle. (1) The air passes over the electric heater. The hot air is then forced out. There are two speeds and three levels of heat – warm, hot and very hot. First of all, (2) make sure your hands are dry. Select the speed and heat settings you want by turning the arrow. Hold the drier about 10cm from your hair and switch the machine on. (3) Use your styling brush to style your hair. Finally, (4) switch the machine off.

Add these four clauses to the paragraph by matching them with positions 1–4. Then write the paragraph out in full in your notebook.

☐ when your hair is dry ...

☐ in order to avoid electrocution ...

☐ as you move the drier over your hair ...

☐ as air is drawn into the drier ...

Complete this passage about a solar cooker. Use the words and phrases in this list.

| is placed | in order to | if | is used for | are reflected | avoid | when |
| begins | and so | must be turned | consists of |

A solar cooker (a)_____ cooking in dry, sunny countries. It is particularly useful in

countries where fuel is expensive. It (b)_____ a curved mirror with a stand fixed to

the middle of the mirror. The cooker is set up in an open space facing the sun. The mirror

is curved, (c)_____ the sun's rays (d)_____ by the mirror and concentrated onto

the stand. (e)_____ a pan containing water (f)_____ on the stand, it becomes hot.

As the pot gets hotter and hotter, the water (g)_____ to boil. (h)_____

get maximum heat, the mirror (i)_____ from time to time so that it continues to

face the sun. (j)_____ the food is ready, the pan must be removed carefully. To

(k)_____ getting burnt while removing the pan, the cook must make sure the mirror is

not facing the sun.

22 Read these sentences about a camera. Put them in the correct order (the first and last sentences are already in position). Then write the paragraph out in full in your notebook.

How a camera works

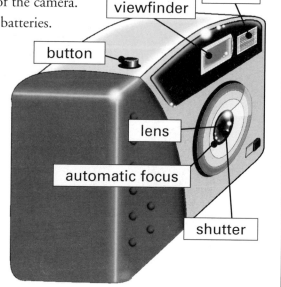

1. This automatic camera is very simple to use.
    a. When you are ready, press the button on the top of the camera.
    b. The film winder and the flash are powered by the batteries.
    c. If there is not enough light, the flash will operate automatically as you take the picture.
    d. You can then see what the picture will look like.
    e. At the end you must make sure that the film is wound on.
    f. It consists of a lens, a button, a viewfinder, a flash and an automatic focus.
    g. Inside the camera is a film and two batteries.
    h. In order to take a photograph, look through the viewfinder.
    i. This opens the shutter and lets in the right amount of light.
11. The camera is now ready for the next picture.

viewfinder · flash · button · lens · automatic focus · shutter

Free writing

 23 Read the paragraph about mobile phones on page 14 again. Now look at the diagram below. Explain what happens when you phone someone with a mobile phone from an ordinary telephone. Use your notebook.

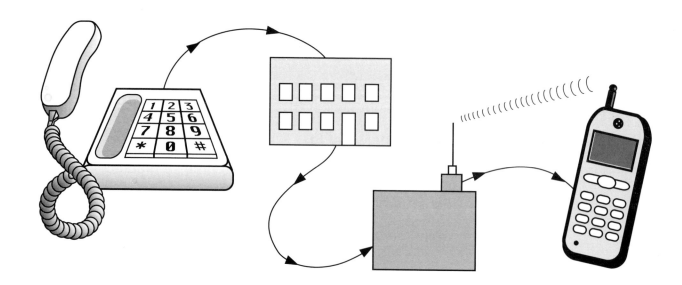

24 Explain how a steamer is used to cook food. Look at this diagram to help you. Use your notebook.

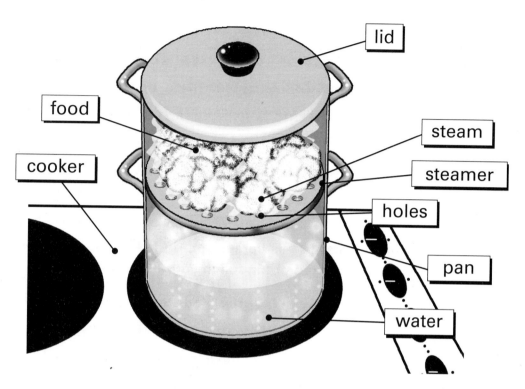

25 Write a paragraph in your notebook about an instrument or electrical appliance that you own – for example a calculator, an alarm clock, a radio or a pager. Draw a diagram of the instrument and explain what it consists of and how it works. When you have finished, show it to someone else in the class to read.

Use this checklist to edit your writing in Exercises 23–25.

CHECKLIST	Exercise		
	23	24	25
How many sentences are there?			
How many full stops (.) are there?			
Does every sentence begin with a capital letter?			
Does every sentence have a verb?			
Have you checked your spelling?			
Can you make your writing **better**?			

Editing

26 **Check this paragraph for spelling, punctuation and capital letters. There are ten mistakes. Write the corrected paragraph out in full in your notebook.**

water-wheels are a very old form of water power They can be maid of wood or metal. They are found in many countrys of the world. For example, the city of Hama, in syria, is famous for it's 17 wooden water-wheels. Water-wheels are usualy located on fast-flowing river's or streams. as the river flows the wheel is turned by the power of the water. The power is used to take watre from the river for farming.

27 **There are ten grammatical mistakes in this paragraph. Underline the mistakes and correct them. Then write the paragraph out in full in your notebook.**

A computer it is a very powerful instrument. Some computers are heavy and is placed on desks. Other computers are quite small and can carried in the pocket. A computer have many different uses. Information are given to the computer and a set of instructions, called a programme. The computer is tell what to do by the programme. A computer is consists of a monitor with a screen, a keyboard, a disk drive, speakers and a mouse. The keyboard and the mouse are using for getting information into the computer. The 'output' it is shown on computer screen.

Vocabulary building

Instruction verbs

28 **Match the instruction verbs with the drawings.**

> press   push   wait   switch off   remove   listen   lift   cut

Parts of an instrument

29 **Label this diagram of a computer. Use these words:**

> screen monitor keyboard speaker disk disk drive
> mouse printer joystick camera

30 **Look at the questions below. The missing words are all found in this unit. Write the answers in the puzzle below and find the vertical word. It is the name of a famous city in the Middle East.**

a. In _____ to record a message, speak into the microphone.
b. An _____ receives signals from telephones.
c. The machine _____ be switched off when it is cleaned.
d. A _____ phone is another word for a mobile phone.
e. Light is let into a camera through a _____.
f. Juice is _____ in a juice jug.
g. In an extractor, juice is separated from the _____.
h. To _____ the volume, use the volume control knob.

a.   <u>o</u>   <u>r</u>   <u>d</u>   <u>e</u>   <u>r</u>

b.   ___   ___   ___   ___   ___   ___

c.   ___   ___   ___   ___

d. ___   ___   ___   ___   ___   ___   ___   ___

e.   ___   ___   ___   ___

f.   ___   ___   ___   ___   ___   ___   ___   ___

g.   ___   ___   ___   ___

h.   ___   ___   ___   ___   ___   ___

Looking at text

1 **Read this paragraph about how hummus is made.**

HUMMUS

Hummus is a very popular dish in Greece, Turkey and many parts of the Arab world. It <u>is made</u> from chickpeas and sesame-seed paste and it is very easy to make. First of all, the chickpeas <u>have to be soaked</u> for several hours. Then they <u>are drained</u> and placed in a pressure cooker. They are covered with water and a teaspoon of bicarbonate of soda is added. They are steamed for about 20 minutes until they are soft. The chickpeas are then drained and the juice is kept. A few chickpeas are put on one side for a garnish. The rest of them are put into a blender and some of the juice is added. The chickpeas are mixed in the blender until a soft puree is formed. As the chickpeas are mixed, salt, crushed garlic and *tahina* paste are all added. Finally, lemon juice is added. By this time the mixture should be smooth and creamy. In order to serve the hummus, the mixture is poured into a dish, olive oil is added and the extra chickpeas and an olive are placed on top. Paprika and chopped parsley can be added as decoration around the edge of the dish. Hummus is usually served at room temperature with hot bread.

Put the pictures below in the correct order by numbering them 1–6. Then write these past participles under the correct pictures.

> poured   drained   soaked   steamed   served   mixed

A   B   C   D   E   F

2 **Look at the paragraph again. Underline the passive verbs. The first three have been done for you.**

3 | **Language:** sequence words

| When we describe the steps in how we make something we use **sequence words** such as: |||||||||
| first | first of all | then | now | next | meanwhile | after that | lastly | finally |

Circle the sequence words in the paragraph about hummus.

4 **Underline the following in the paragraph about hummus:**

a. two *until* clauses
b. one *as* clause
c. the phrase *in order to*

5 **Read this passage about building roads.**

Building a road

The Irohazaka Driveway in Japan is famous for its wonderful views. The road, which was named after a poem by a 9th. century Buddhist monk, takes visitors to the Kegon Waterfalls near Tokyo. It cuts through high mountains and has a total of 48 very sharp 'hairpin' bends. It is a marvellous engineering project. But how can such a road be built? Where do the road engineers begin?

First of all, a lot of planning is needed. Surveys and aerial photos are used in order to choose the best route. Then the route is marked out on the ground by the surveyors. Earth-moving machines are then used to make the route as flat as possible. Cuttings are made through hills and valleys are filled in with rock and earth. Bridges and tunnels may also be needed. When the route is ready, the foundations of the road can be laid using crushed rock. After that a layer of concrete is put on top of the foundations. A machine called a spreader then adds the top surface layer, which consists either of concrete or asphalt. The latter is a dark, sticky substance produced from petroleum. Lastly, road markings must be painted on the road surface and road signs added.

a. Circle the sequence words.

b. Underline the passive verbs.

c. What are surveys and aerial photos used for?

   They are _____

d. Who marks the route out?

   The route is _____

e. When can the foundations of the road be laid?

   The foundations can _____

f. What are added to the road at the end? _____

6 ## Language: *by* after a passive verb

> **Look at these sentences:**
>
> The route is marked out **by** the surveyors.   Hummus is made **by mixing** chickpeas with …

> ***By*** after a passive verb can tell us **who** does something (the surveyors) or **how** something is done (by mixing …).

Read about rubber production. Then answer the questions below.

——— Producing natural rubber ———

Rubber is a natural substance, although it can also be made synthetically. Natural rubber is made from a white liquid called latex, which is produced by rubber trees. This liquid is collected by cutting a small piece of bark from the tree. It runs slowly into a cup which is attached to the tree. After a few hours the latex stops flowing.

All of the cups are emptied and the latex is taken to the rubber factory. The latex is poured into large tanks where it is solidified by adding acid. The rubber forms thick strips, which are then flattened by passing through rollers and turned into thin sheets. They are then packed and exported to countries all over the world.

---

a. What produces latex? _____

b. How is latex collected?

_____

c. How is the liquid latex made solid?

_____

d. How are the strips of solid rubber flattened?

_____

Sentence building

 7 **Add these passive sentences to the table on page 32. Put them in the correct order first. They all contain the form *by …~ing*.**

a. made / sesame-seed paste / together / is / chickpeas / hummus / mixing / and / by

b. speaking / the microphone / recorded / into / a message / is / by

c. are / seat-belts / wearing / drivers / their / protected / by

31

What?	(Passive) Verb	How?	.
The liquid	is collected	by cutting a small piece of bark from the tree	.

8 Complete these sentences using *by ...~ing.*

 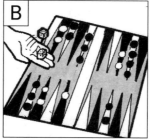  

a. The potatoes are softened by _____

b. In backgammon, the pieces are moved by _____

c. The gates are opened automatically by _____

d. The colour green is made by _____

Joining ideas

9 **Language:** *also*

Look at the position of *also* in these sentences:

Rubber is **also** used for making diving suits.

Hummus can **also** be bought in cans.

Maria **also** studies Computer Science.

Now complete the rule:

Also comes _____ verbs like *is* and _____. It comes _____ the main verb.

Write out the second sentence in each pair in your notebook. Add *also* in the correct position.

a. Sardines are a popular fish in Portugal. They are found in other parts of the world.

b. Rubber trees are grown in plantations in Southeast Asia. They grow naturally in the Amazon region of Brazil.

c. The cursor is moved around the computer screen by using the arrows on the keyboard. It can be moved by clicking the mouse.

d. Kiri Te Kanawa is a famous opera singer from New Zealand. She sings popular music.

10 **Write sentences with *also* for each of the sentences below. Use your notebook.**

> Example: *Shark meat is sold in fish markets. It can also be bought in some supermarkets.*

a. My sister likes reading poetry. She ...

b. New York is an important business centre.

c. *Al Akhram* is a well-known newspaper in Egypt.

d. Aeroflot flies all over Asia.

e. Coconuts are grown in the Caribbean.

f. Oil can be used for manufacturing plastics.

11 Language: *which* clauses

Look at these sentences:

The road cuts through high mountains.   The road is named after a poem.

We can join these two ideas using a ***which*** clause.

What?	*Which* clause	Verb + ...
a) The road,	which is named after a poem,	cuts through high mountains.

A ***which*** clause can also be at the end of a sentence.

What?	Verb + ...	*Which* clause
b) The road	cuts through high mountains,	which are over 1,500m in places.

Note that ***which*** refers to the noun that it follows. In a) above it follows *the road*, but in b) it follows *mountains*.

Write these two sentences in the tables on page 33. Remember the commas!

a. Tehran which is the capital of Iran is located in the centre of the country.

b. *Satay* is a simple and delicious dish which is popular throughout South East Asia.

⑫ Find *which* clauses in these paragraphs and underline them.

a. Unit one, pages 1–2, the paragraphs by Salah and Yoko.

b. Unit one, page 3, the paragraph about Kuwait Towers

c. Unit two, page 14, 'A mobile phone'

d. This unit, pages 30 and 31, 'Building a road' and 'Producing natural rubber'

How many *which* clauses did you find? _____

⑬ Join these sentences using *which* clauses. Follow this pattern:

What?	***Which* clause**	**Verb + ...**

a. Indonesia has a population of more than 200 million people. Indonesia consists of nearly 14,000 islands.

_____

b. Rubber is grown in tropical countries such as Malaysia. Rubber needs a hot, humid climate.

_____

c. The Panama Canal is just over 64 km long. It connects the Pacific and Atlantic Oceans.

_____

d. A fax machine is an important part of a modern office. A fax machine works by sending printed material through telephone lines.

_____

_____

e. The *erhu* has only two strings. It is a Chinese instrument rather like a Western violin.

_____

_____

14 **Join these sentences using *which* clauses. Follow this pattern:**

What?	Verb + ...	*Which* clause

a. An answering machine records messages. The messages can then be played back when you get home.

_____

b. My brother has just bought a Nissan Patrol. A Nissan Patrol is one of the most popular four-wheel-drive vehicles in the world.

_____

_____

c. Last week we visited Petra. Petra is the most famous historical site in Jordan.

_____

d. The surface of the road is then sprayed with asphalt. Asphalt is a dark, sticky substance produced from petroleum.

_____

_____

e. Strips of rubber are passed through rollers. The rollers flatten the strips and produce thin sheets.

_____

15 **Language: *although* clauses**

Although Pepe is quite intelligent, ... | he doesn't know how to set the video recorder!

35

Although clause	**Last part of the sentence**
Although Pepe is quite intelligent,	he doesn't know how to set his video recorder.
First part of the sentence	***Although* clause**
Pepe doesn't know how to set his video recorder,	although he is quite intelligent.

Although clauses can go at the beginning or the end of a sentence. Note the position of the commas.

Find and underline *although* clauses in these paragraphs:

a. Unit one, page 1, the paragraphs by Maria and Salah

b. This unit, page 31, 'Producing natural rubber'

16 **Match the *although* clauses with the main sentences. Write out the complete sentences in your notebook. Remember the commas!**

a. Although fishermen have the money to buy modern boats

b. Although the car is eight years old

c. Although Egypt has very low rainfall

d. Although the computer is quite powerful

e. Although it can be very cold in Hong Kong in the winter

f. Although those watches are very cheap

g. Although some perfumes are made in India

... the modem is rather slow.

... it never snows.

... most are imported from France.

... they are also very attractive.

... they often prefer to use the old wooden ones.

... many crops can be grown using irrigation.

... it is in excellent condition.

17 **Complete these sentences.**

a. Although I like television, _____

b. Although I understand Cantonese, _____

c. Although Anita is only four years old, _____

d. Although Singapore is only a group of small islands, _____

Write two more sentences about yourself or your city in your notebook. Use *although* clauses.

Punctuation

 Punctuate these sentences. They all contain *which* or *although* clauses.

a. although the suitcase is very large it only weighs 6kg

b. my new cassette players got two tape decks which is very useful for copying tapes

c. buenos aires which is the capital of argentina is situated on the river plate

d. yoko sends e-mail messages all the time although she found computers difficult to use at first

e. last summer we flew to singapore on qantas which is an australian airline

f. although toyota is a japanese company toyota cars are built in many different countries

g. the carnival in rio which takes place in february every year attracts thousands of visitors from all over the world

h. a juice extractor can be used for most types of fruit and vegetables although it is not very suitable for oranges and lemons

Better paragraphs

 Read this paragraph describing how to make *blinis*.

This is a recipe for blinis. They are quite easy to prepare and very filling. (1) About 140 g of buckwheat flour is measured and poured into a bowl. Baking powder, salt and an egg are (2) added and mixed together. (3) About 150 ml of milk and 3 tablespoons of yoghurt are added and beaten into the mixture. The mixture is (4) left on one side for a few minutes. (5) Heat a little butter in a large pan. Add a tablespoon of the mixture. When the blini is brown on the bottom, it should be turned over and cooked for another minute. The blinis must be kept warm until they are all ready. (6) Serve the blinis. Most people prefer to eat them with sour cream and caviar.

a. Add these sequence words to the paragraph by matching them with positions 1–6.

☐ also ☐ also ☐ finally ☐ first of all ☐ then ☐ meanwhile

b. Show where you can add the following *which* clause to the paragraph:

> which are small, flat pancakes popular in Russia

c. Now add this *although* clause:

> they can be eaten on their own or with jam

d. Write the 'better' paragraph out in full in your notebook.

20 **Complete this paragraph about sugar-cane. Use the words and phrases in this list.**

> if   although   which   which   in order to   when   until   as

Sugar-cane is a tall grass, similar to bamboo, (a)_____ grows mainly in hot, wet countries. (b)_____ it needs a lot of water, it can grow in areas of low rainfall such as Egypt. There must, however, be plenty of irrigation water. Small pieces of cane are planted in the fields and soon begin to grow. (c)_____ they are growing, the cane fields have to be weeded all the time. (d)_____ the cane is fully grown, it is cut a few centimetres above ground level. Sometimes the fields are burnt first (e)_____ burn off the leaves. (f)_____ the fields are not burnt, the leaves must be cut by hand. The cane is taken to the sugar factories. Here the cane is cut again into small lengths. It is then passed through a crushing machine, (g) _____ extracts all the juice. The juice is then boiled (h)_____ crystals of sugar are formed.

21 **Look at the sentences on page 39.**

a. Put the verbs into the passive form (*to be* + past participle).

b. Put the sentences in the correct order to make a paragraph. The first sentence is already in place.

c. Write out the complete paragraph in your notebook.

NEW TOWNS

1. The population of many areas of the world is growing rapidly.

a. Electric power and water _____ (bring) to the site and drains _____ (dig).

b. Before building can begin, the land _____ (map) by surveyors.

c. Finally, trees and gardens _____ (plant) to make the town more attractive.

d. Aerial and satellite photos _____ also _____ (need).

e. Then architects, planners and engineers look at the maps, and plans _____ (draw up) for the new town.

f. When everyone has agreed on the plans, work can begin.

g. Then buildings, such as houses, apartment blocks, schools and shops _____ (construct).

h. The new towns _____ usually _____ (build) in rural areas.

i. As a result there is a great need for new towns; one example is Shatin in the Hong Kong region of China.

j. First of all roads _____ (lay).

Free writing

 Read the paragraph about making hummus on page 29 again. Now look at these notes for making *crème caramel*. Write a paragraph in your notebook describing how it is prepared. Use passive verbs. Begin like this:

Crème caramel is delicious and easy to prepare. It is popular all over the world. The caramel is usually made before the custard. First of all the sugar is heated in a saucepan and stirred gently from time to time ...

Ingredients: For the caramel: 175 g of white 'caster' sugar
                                     Two tablespoons of hot water

                For the custard: 150 ml milk

                                     275 ml of cream

                                     4 large eggs

                                     1 teaspoon of pure vanilla extract

1. heat the sugar in a saucepan
2. stir gently
3. remove from heat (when sugar is brown liquid)
4. add water carefully
5. pour ⅔ of caramel into bottom of a dish
6. make custard – add milk and cream to remaining ⅓ of caramel in the saucepan
7. heat gently and mix
8. mix eggs in a large bowl
9. add mixture from the pan – mix
10. add vanilla extract
11. pour into dish
12. bake in oven for 1¼ hours
13. remove from oven and allow to cool
14. place in refrigerator for several hours
15. serve with cream

23 Use these pictures to write a paragraph in your notebook about the process of building a skyscraper.

surveying

drawing up the plans

building the framework

skyscraper

laying the foundations

24 Think of a dish or a drink that you like. Describe how it is prepared. Use your notebook.

Use this checklist to edit your writing in Exercises 22–24.

CHECKLIST	Exercise		
	22	23	24
How many sentences are there?			
How many full stops (.) are there?			
Does every sentence begin with a capital letter?			
Does every sentence have a verb?			
Have you checked your spelling?			
Can you make your writing **better**?			

Editing

25 Check the verbs in this paragraph about cotton production. There are eight mistakes. Write the corrected paragraph out in full in your notebook.

Cotton is grow in hot areas such as Egypt and parts of China. It needs plenty of water, either from rainfall or from irrigation, and good, rich soils. When the cotton will be ready, it must harvested quickly before rain can damage it. The cotton are sometimes picked by hand, but usually it is picked by machines. The cotton is collect and placed in machines, where the fibres (called 'lint') are separating from the cotton seeds. The lint is then packed into bales and send to factories where cotton cloth are manufactured.

26 Look at this advertisement for the Paradise Restaurant. There are 12 mistakes in spelling, punctuation and capital letters. Underline the mistakes and correct them. Then write the paragraph out in full in your notebook.

WELCOME TO PARADISE!

Do you like delicious, spicy food servd in beautiful surroundings? Yes? Then visit our new 'paradise Restaurant'. We are locatd in Ocean Avenue in the centre of the city Our restaurant which has wonderful views of the city, is on the tetnh

floor of the Toyota Tower. The menu, wich is prepared by our experienced chef contains Chinese, malaysian and Indonesian dishes. Although our prices are low you will find that the quality of the food is very haigh. Come and visit us soon!

Paradise Restaurant

Vocabulary building

Describing construction

27 Look at the table on page 43. Match the verbs on the left with the nouns across the top. Put ✓ in the correct boxes and ✗ in the incorrect ones. For example, you can build a bridge, but you cannot build an omelette. Some of the verbs match more than one noun.

	a bridge	a well	the foundations	a plan	a hole	an omelette
build	✓					✗
draw up						
lay						
construct						
make						
drill						
dig						

Describing recipes

28 **Match these verbs with the diagrams below.**

> drain   mix   boil   heat   add   pour   steam   measure   cover

 A

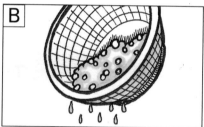 B

 C

_____   _____   _____

 D

 E

 F

_____   _____   _____

 G

 H

 I

_____   _____   _____

Describing processes

29 **We use the verbs below when we describe how things are processed. Match the verbs with the pictures.**

> transport   cut   plant   collect   pick   pass through
> pour into   spray   export

_____   _____   _____

_____   _____   _____

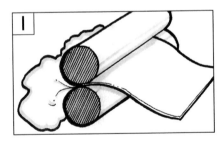

_____   _____   _____

Irregular past participles

30 **Look at the irregular past participles in the table below.**

INFINITIVE	PAST SIMPLE	PAST PARTICIPLE
to put	put	**put**
to buy	bought	**bought**
to grow	grew	**grown**

Now put the correct past participle into each of these sentences.

a. Sugar-cane can be _____ by machine or by hand. (cut)

b. Most electrical goods are _____ in Asia. (make)

c. First, the drains have to be _____. (dig)

d. When the ground is flat, the foundations are _____. (lay)

e. Skyscrapers are usually _____ in the centre of cities, where land is expensive. (build)

f. Signals are _____ by mobile phones to special aerials. (send)

g. Photographs must be _____ of the site of the new town. (take)

h. Plans are usually _____ up by architects, engineers and planners. (draw)

i. Some planets can be _____ in the night sky without a telescope. (see)

j. Natural rubber trees are _____ in many parts of the world. (find)

Reporting what someone said

Looking at text

1 **Read Victor's story. He is explaining what happened to him on a boat trip. Choose a picture to go with the story.**

I <u>had</u> an awful experience a few days ago. I went fishing with Carlos, who is a good friend of mine. We were in Carlos's motor boat. Although it <u>had rained</u> in the morning, it was a fine, sunny afternoon. The boat was quite fast and after travelling for about an hour, land was out of sight. We <u>were heading</u> for an old wreck, which was a favourite fishing spot. Suddenly the engine <u>stopped</u>. Silence. 'What's happened?' I asked Carlos. 'We've run out of petrol,' he replied. I was beginning to feel a bit nervous and I asked him what we were going to do. He told me not to worry. 'We've got some petrol in this spare can,' he said as he lifted a metal container from the bottom of the boat. He opened the can. Now he looked worried too. I asked him what was wrong. 'It's empty,' he said. 'My nephew used the boat yesterday, and he probably forgot to fill up the spare can,' he explained. We looked all around us, but there were no boats in sight. There were some dark clouds on the horizon, and in the distance I could hear thunder.

2 **Write answers to these questions.**

a. What were Carlos and Victor heading for in the boat?

They _____

b. What happened to the engine? *It* _____

c. Why did Carlos look worried?

Because _____

d. Who had used the boat the previous day?

_____

3 **Language:** telling a story

When we tell a story we use verbs in the **past simple** tense to describe an action that took place at a specific point in the past:

| I **had** an awful experience a few days ago. | Suddenly, the engine **stopped**. |

We use the **past continuous** tense to describe an action that continued over a period of time in the past and that was taking place when another action took place:

We **were heading** for an old wreck when suddenly the engine stopped.

We use the **past perfect** tense to describe something that happened before the story began:

Though it **had rained** in the morning, it was a fine, sunny afternoon.

Look at Victor's story again.

a. Find five regular verbs and five irregular verbs in the past simple tense. Write them below.

Regular: *stopped,* _____

Irregular: *had,* _____

b. Find one more past continuous verb.

were heading, _____

c. Find a *which* clause, an *as* clause and an *although* clause. Underline them.

d. Find one clause that begins with *who*. Underline it.

 4 **Language:** reporting verbs

We use verbs such as *say, tell, ask, reply, explain,* etc. to report what someone said.

'What's happened?' I **asked** Carlos.

'We've run out of petrol,' he **replied**.

'We've got some petrol in this spare can,' he **said**.

Language: direct and indirect speech

Look at these examples:

a) Carlos said, 'I feel cold.'   b) Carlos said (**that**) he felt cold.

Example a) is **direct** speech. Example b) is **indirect** speech. What are the four things that are different in b)?

Underline the verbs in the direct and indirect speech in these sentences. How are the tenses different?

a. Carlos said, 'My nephew borrowed the boat.'

b. Carlos said that his nephew had borrowed the boat.

c. 'I've never run out of petrol before,' Carlos said.

d. Carlos said that he had never run out of petrol before.

e. I said, 'It's going to rain.'

f. I said that it was going to rain.

g. 'I can't swim,' I said.

h. I said that I couldn't swim.

5 **Read Christina's story. Find out where Christina and Sonia live.**

An interesting thing happened to me last year. I flew to Miami with my family for three weeks. We were staying in an apartment not far from downtown Miami. One evening we went for a walk to the harbour, Bayside, which was not far from the apartment. My uncle, who knows Miami very well, wanted to take us to have some Cuban food. Suddenly I saw an old friend, Sonia. It was a wonderful surprise. I hadn't seen her since I left school in Salvador six years ago. I had heard that she had got married and had gone to live in Belo Horizonte. After greeting each other, I asked her if she was still living in Belo Horizonte. 'No', she said, 'my husband got a job in Rio de Janeiro. We have been there for two years.' I told her that I also lived in Rio. 'We bought an apartment there last month,' I said. Sonia asked me which part of Rio I lived in. I explained that the apartment was in the suburbs, opposite a football stadium. 'Is it a very large building with blue balconies?' asked Sonia. I told her that it was. I was rather surprised, and asked her how she knew the building so well. 'We live in the same building!' she explained.

a. Find three examples of direct speech and underline them.

b. Find three examples of indirect speech and underline them.

c. Put a circle around four different reporting verbs.

d. Find an example of a past continuous verb (*was/were* + *~ing*).

e. Find an example of a past perfect verb (*had* + past participle).

6 **Add these reporting verbs to the sentences below:**

> said   told   explained   replied

a. I _____ Sonia that I also lived in Rio.

b. I _____ that my husband had been offered a new job at the university and we had decided to move there a few months ago.

c. 'How do you like Rio?' asked Sonia. 'It's great,' I _____.

d. Sonia _____ that she liked it too. They hoped to stay there for many years.

7 **Read this newspaper report. What are the people in the pictures saying? Change the reported speech into direct speech and put it into the captions.**

BOMBAY PLANE CRASH

An aeroplane that was trying to land at Bombay airport crashed into the sea yesterday. Fortunately all the passengers were rescued. Many had cuts and bruises and some had to go to hospital. The plane was flying from Amman to Bombay.

Ahmed Said, who was going to visit relatives in India, said that he was reading when he heard a loud bang. 'I looked out of the window,' Ahmed explained, 'and saw smoke. I told the stewardess that one of the engines was on fire. Then the pilot spoke to the passengers over the intercom system. He told us that we were going to land in the sea. The stewardess told us to put on our lifejackets,' said Ahmed, 'and after that I began to pray.' Ahmed explained what had happened after landing on the water. 'Everything was very quiet for a few seconds,' he said, 'and then everyone got up and went towards the emergency exits, which were now open. From there we could see the water a few metres below. Fortunately it was calm and we got into the rescue boats safely.'

A spokeswoman for International Air said that it was their first accident. 'We don't know what caused the engine to explode. It's a mystery,' she said.

8 **Read these sentences from the newspaper article. What (or who) do the underlined words refer to?**

a. Fortunately all the passengers were rescued. <u>Many</u> had cuts and bruises and <u>some</u> had to go to hospital. _____

b. Then the pilot spoke to the passengers ... <u>He</u> told <u>us</u> that we were going to land in the sea. _____

c. Everyone got up and went towards the emergency exits, which were now open. From <u>there</u> we could see the water a few metres below. _____

d. A spokeswoman for International Air said that it was <u>their</u> first accident.

_____

Sentence building

 These sentences all contain indirect speech. Put the words in the correct order and write them in the table below.

a. that / said / cancelled / teacher / the / was / the / class

b. late / she / Olga / us / be / told / that / would

c. that / with / there / engine / was / said / the / the / a problem / pilot

d. policeman / drive / carefully / told / more / me / the / to

e. said / had / week / Sunil / his cousin / the car / that / used / last

Who	*said/told (me)*	*(that)*	Indirect speech	.
Sonia	said	that	she had moved there last year	.

10 **Report these statements using *said* or *told me/us*.**

a. *Janet said* _____

b. *Our teacher told us* _____

c. *The man* _____

d. *Sam* _____

11 | **Language:** reported questions |

A *yes/no* **question** is reported like this:

Anne asked, 'Do you like music?'	Anne asked me **if** I like**d** music.

A *wh* **question** is reported like this:

Keiko asked: 'Where do you live?'	Keiko asked me **where** I live**d**.

Where is a question word. Other question words are ***when, why, how, what, who,*** etc.

Write these as reported (or indirect) questions in the table below.

a. The doctor: 'Are you feeling better?'   c. Pierre: 'Do you speak French?'

b. Aziz: 'When do you have your lunch break?'   d. The waiter: 'What do you want to drink?'

Who?	asked (me)	if	Indirect question	.
Anne	asked me	if	I liked music	.

Who?	asked (me)	Question word	Indirect question	.
Keiko	asked me	where	I lived	.

Joining ideas

 Language: *after/before ...~ing*

Look at these sentences:	
The plane lost an engine.	The plane crashed into the sea.

We can join these sentences with **after:**	
After the plane lost an engine, it crashed into the sea. OR	**After losing an engine,** the plane crashed into the sea.

We can also join sentences with **before**:	
Mei Lin read the instructions.	Mei Lin switched on the machine.
Before Mei Lin switched on the machine, OR she read the instructions.	**Before switching on the machine,** Mei Lin read the instructions.

Now join these sentences using *after/before ...~ing* and write them in your notebook. Remember the commas.

a. John had a large lunch. John fell asleep for twenty minutes. (after)

b. Make sure you check that there is enough petrol. Start the boat. (before)

c. We lived in Rome for six years. We moved to Istanbul. (after)

d. Nina tried on the dress. Nina bought the dress. (before)

e. Mike wrote the letter. Mike faxed the letter to the head office in Cairo. (after)

f. Ibn Batuta visited Mecca. Ibn Batuta travelled to China. (before)

Language: *who* clauses

Who **clauses** tell us something extra about a person (or people). They can come in the middle of a sentence:

Dr Martinez has been a lecturer in the college for many years.

Dr Martinez is the new head of the department.

Who?	*Who* clause	Last part of the sentence
Dr Martinez,	who is the new head of the department,	has been a lecturer in the college for many years.

Who **clauses** can also come at the end of a sentence.

I went shopping with my cousin.

My cousin is staying with me for a few weeks.

First part of the sentence	Who?	*Who* clause
I went shopping with	my cousin,	who is staying with me for a few weeks.

Now join these sentences in the same way in your notebook. Remember the commas.

a. Ronaldo scored six goals last week. Ronaldo is an excellent football player.

b. I've just had a phone call from my sister. My sister is studying at a college in Manila.

c. The mechanic said he could repair the car by the following day. The mechanic was very experienced.

d. This morning I went to see the doctor. The doctor said I should rest for three days.

e. Mohsin is reading a book about Atatürk. Atatürk was the founder of modern Turkey.

f. Our English teacher is probably the best teacher in the college. Our English teacher is very kind, hard-working and helpful.

Add your own *who* clauses to these sentences. They are all about famous people. Use your notebook.

a. Ibn Batuta travelled to many countries, including Spain, Russia and China.

b. I've just been listening to some music by Paul McCartney.

c. Gandi died in India in 1948.

d. One of the richest men in the world is Bill Gates.

e. Mrs Thatcher was Prime Minister of the United Kingdom from 1979 to 1990.

f. Omar Khayam is most famous as the author of the *Rubaiyat*.

Now write three sentences about people you know. Use *who* clauses.

a. _____

b. _____

c. _____

Punctuation

 These sentences all contain *who* clauses. Add commas, full stops and capital letters if they are needed.

a. the pathans who come from the mountainous regions of pakistan speak pashto as their mother tongue

b. anna who has just graduated from the university of singapore wants to be an economist

c. the druze are a religious sect who live mainly in the mountainous regions of lebanon and southern syria

d. my uncle who doesn't speak a word of english told me that he is planning to visit america in the summer

e. yesterday I went to visit my grandmother who is in hospital with a chest complaint

f. italians who are well-known for their love of music have some of the world's greatest opera singers

 Punctuate these sentences containing *after* and *before*.

a. after walking for six miles in the hot sun the man finally found a garage

b. before cooking the sardines they washed them and cut them into pieces

c. after landing in the sea and waiting for the rescue boats the passengers finally escaped

d. before going on a boat trip make sure that there is petrol in the spare can

Study the direct speech in the earlier paragraphs and in the example below.

> *'What's happened?' I asked Carlos.*
>
> *'We've run out of petrol,' he replied.*

Now punctuate these sentences.

a. id like a single room he told the receptionist

b. whats the time *carlos* asked six oclock I replied

c. follow the london road and turn left at the roundabout explained tania

d. its very hot today said boris I think ill go for a swim

54

Better paragraphs

 Read this paragraph about a children's birthday party.

On Saturday Gabriella invited me to her house. She was having a small party for her daughter, Elena. My father offered to take me in his car and I arrived about two o'clock. The house was full of people. There was a lot of noise from the children. Gabriella asked me if I wanted to meet Elena's teacher. I said 'Yes,' and so she took me into the garden and I was introduced to Koula. Gabriella brought us both some orange juice and cake. I want to be a teacher too, and so I asked Koula many questions about teaching. She told me that she had studied at a teacher's training college in Thessaloniki. After leaving teacher training college, she went to teach in a small village school. Three years ago she moved to the city and started teaching at Elena's school. I asked her what she liked most about teaching. 'The children,' she replied, 'they are lovely.' At that moment, the ball landed on the table and knocked the cake and orange juice onto the ground. 'Well, most of the time,' she added with a smile.

Now add this 'extra information' to the paragraph. Then write the paragraph out in full in your notebook.

a. who is a very close friend of mine

b. who doesn't work on Saturdays

c. which was quite large

d. who were playing with a plastic beach ball.

e. who was sitting under a tree

f. which she had baked for Elena's party

g. which is a large city to the north-east of Athens

h. which is only half a kilometre from her home

19   **Use these words to complete the paragraph:**

> before   which   in order to   if   when   that   although   after   who   who

The famous 5,000-metre runner Naseem Ahmed arrived in Tunis today. Naseem,

(a)_____ was born in Yemen but now lives in Germany, was met at the airport

by many fans and journalists. He told the crowd (b)_____ he was very happy to be

in Tunisia, (c)_____ he was sorry that it was only a short visit. Naseem has

come to Tunisia (d)_____ take part in the African Championship,

(e)_____ starts tomorrow. (f)_____ visiting Tunis, Naseem will travel to

Morocco, (g)_____ returning to Germany at the end of the month. One

journalist asked him (h)_____ he thought he would win the race. 'I'm not sure,'

he replied, 'there are a lot of good runners in the race. It'll be hard.' Naseem,

(i)_____ is well known for his modesty and good sportsmanship, became famous

(j)_____ he won an Olympic gold medal for the 5,000 metres two years ago.

20   **A joke! Put the sentences in paragraphs A and C in the correct order. Then write them out in full in your notebook.**

Three Sailors and a Genie

Paragraph A

a. The sailors were astonished and stared at the genie in disbelief.

b. One day they saw a bottle floating in the water.

c. They ate only raw fish and coconuts and after many months they were becoming very thin and weak.

d. There was a flash of light and suddenly a genie jumped out of the bottle.

e. Many years ago three sailors were shipwrecked on a small desert island in the middle of nowhere.

f. One of the sailors picked it up and took out the cork.

Paragraph B

The genie bowed and spoke to them. 'I am the genie of the bottle,' he said. 'Your wish is my command.' He explained that because they had rescued him they could each ask for a wish. 'Anything we want?' asked the first sailor. 'Yes, anything,' replied the genie.'

Paragraph C

a. Suddenly there was a flash and the first sailor disappeared.

b. He told the genie that he missed his shipmates and he'd like to go back to the ship to join them.

c. 'I'd like my two friends to come back to the island!' he told the genie.

d. Again the genie clapped his hands and the second sailor disappeared.

e. The third sailor, who was now alone, suddenly felt very sad.

f. The genie clapped his hands.

g. The first sailor then explained that he missed his family very much and asked if the genie would send him back home.

h. 'That was marvellous,' said the second sailor.

Free writing

21 Read the story about Victor and Carlos on page 46 again. How did the story end? How did they get back home again? Write a paragraph in your notebook to finish the story. Use the past simple, past continuous and past perfect.

22 Read Christina's paragraph on page 48 again. Now imagine you are Sonia. Write about the meeting with Christina in your notebook. Use some direct and indirect speech.

23 **Imagine you are a reporter. Read this interview with a stewardess who was on the plane that landed in the sea (see page 49). Then write a paragraph about the interview in your notebook. Use some indirect speech. Begin like this:**

After the crash I spoke to Gita, who was one

of the stewardesses on the flight.

Reporter: Are you a stewardess with International Air?

Stewardess: Yes, I am. I've been with them for five years.

Reporter: Can you tell me what happened on the flight?

Stewardess: Well, I was serving coffee when I heard a loud bang. I looked out of the window and saw that one of the engines was on fire.

Reporter: What did you do?

Stewardess: I went to the cockpit and reported the fire to the captain.

Reporter: What happened next?

Stewardess: The captain spoke to the passengers. Then I explained how to put the lifejackets on. I tried to keep everyone calm. Then we hit the water and I helped everyone off the plane and into the boats.

Reporter: Were you afraid?

Stewardess: Not really. I was too busy to think about crashing.

Reporter: Will you fly again?

Stewardess: Yes. In fact, I'm scheduled to fly next week.

24 **Write about an interesting thing that happened to you. What happened? Where were you? Report what you said and what other people said. Use your notebook.**

Use this checklist to edit your writing in Exercises 21–24.

CHECKLIST	Exercise			
	21	22	23	24
How many sentences are there?				
How many full stops (.) are there?				
Does every sentence begin with a capital letter?				
Does every sentence have a verb?				
Have you checked your spelling?				
Can you make your writing **better**?				

Editing

25 Read the beginning of this story. There are five spelling mistakes, five mistakes in punctuation, and five grammatical mistakes. Find the mistakes and correct them. Then write the paragraph out in full in your notebook.

One day last summer my family went for a picnac in a park near the sea. We leave home early in the morning and found a quiet place under some trees We put up the tent, which we always take with us and my sister and I began to prepare some food. After eating, we was all resting near the tint and Somboon, which is my youngest son, was playing with a ball. I told him to go and blay near the trees. A few minutes later he screamed and fell to the ground. We all ran over and found him holding his foet. What's the matter?' I ask. 'Its my foot,' he cried. 'Something bit me.' Then we see a large snake in the grass. I told my husband to kill it quickly. He picked up a stick and hit it hard until it was no longer moving. Then he said he would take somboon to the hospital. We all went with him in the jeep. I was very waried because Somboon was breathing with difficulty.

Vocabulary building

Reporting verbs

26 Find the reporting verbs. They are all in the past tense.

1. i d a s _____   2. d e l i n x a e p _____   3. d o l t _____

4. s e d k a _____   5. d e d a d _____   6. l i d e r p e _____

Describing emotions

27 Make two lists from these adjectives. One for words similar to *worried*, and one for words similar to *calm*.

nervous   relaxed   afraid   tranquil   frightened   confident   concerned
peaceful   anxious   quiet   tense   still

worried _____ _____   calm _____ _____

_____ _____   _____ _____

_____ _____   _____ _____

28 **Use these clues to complete the crossword below. Most of the words are in this unit.**

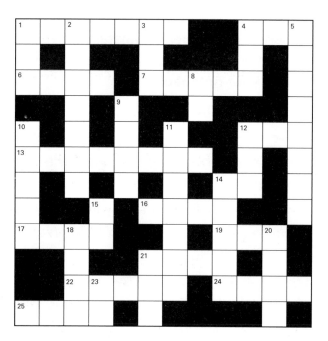

ACROSS

1. The line where the sky meets the sea. (7 letters)
4. 'Would you like ___ or coffee?' the waiter asked. (3)
6. The boys said that they had ___ their homework and so I let them watch TV. (4)
7. Victor and Carlos got into trouble because the spare can was ___. (5)
12. Kiri Te Kanawa, ___ is a famous opera singer, visited Manila a few years ago. (3)
13. My son ___ when the snake bit him. (8)
14. ___ we were walking by the harbour, I met an old friend. (2)
16. To hit the hands together. (4)
17. There were ___ clouds in the distance. I thought it would rain. (4)
19. The stewardess told us to ___ on our lifejackets. (3)
21. 'How do you ___ ?' the doctor asked. 'Terrible,' I replied. (4)
22. Boris told me that he ___ swim very well. (5)
24. Last ___ I visited Turkey. (4)
25. We usually use the past simple tense ___ we tell a story. (4)

DOWN

1. Peter explained that he ___ left the keys to the car in a different jacket. (3)
2. Carl Lewis and Haile Gebreselassie are famous ___. (7)
3. Several passengers were injured and ___ man had to go to hospital. (3)
4. 'I'm going to ___ to land the plane in the sea,' said the pilot. (3)
5. ___ it was a sunny day, the wind was very cold. (8)
8. Prime Minister or afternoon. (2)
9. Hari said ___ he was going to be late for the meeting. (4)
10. Suzanne ___ me if I wanted to go for a walk. (5)
11. I ___ that I was feeling rather tired. (7)
12. I ___ heading for the shop when I saw my friend Anne. (3)
14. In order to ___ for a place at the university, it is necessary to fill in a form. (5)
15. All right! (2)
18. ___, which is grown in Egypt, needs plenty of water and high temperatures. (4)
20. Travelling by plane is safer ___ travelling by car. (4)
21. Salem told me that he was going to ___ to Jakarta next week. (3)
23. Ahmed told the stewardess that the engine was ___ fire. (2)

Looking at text

1 **Kate is writing to Aunt Sarah's problem page in a magazine. Kate has two options. What are they?**

Dear Aunt Sarah

Q I have to make a difficult decision. Next year I want to go to college in order to continue my studies. I'd like to do a teacher training course. However, the college which has the most suitable course is in Exeter, nearly 500 miles from Edinburgh. I like Exeter. It's a lovely city, and it has a good climate. In fact, the climate is better than Edinburgh's. It's warmer in the winter, and it's less windy! But it's smaller than Edinburgh, and I think I would find life less interesting there. It's also a very long way from my family and friends. I think I would be lonely! There's a college which I could go to in Edinburgh. However, it doesn't have the course which I really want to do. What should I do, Aunt Sarah? You're the only person I can ask.

– Kate

2 **Read the letter again and complete the notes in the table below. It shows the points for and against Exeter.**

FOR	AGAINST
lovely town	smaller than Edinburgh

3   **Read Aunt Sarah's reply. What is her advice?**

A Dear Kate,

It's always difficult to make a decision like this. On the one hand, you don't want to leave your family and friends in Edinburgh, but on the other hand, the most suitable course for you is in Exeter. Personally, I think you should go to study in Exeter. It sounds like a lovely place to me. I agree, too, that the winters there are more comfortable than in Edinburgh, which sometimes seems the coldest place in the world when the east wind is blowing!

However, the climate is not the most important thing. You must take the course which is best for you. In this case, we know that the most suitable course is in Exeter. Although you'll miss your family at first, I think you'll soon make new friends in Exeter. Is there a flight from Exeter to Edinburgh? If there is, you can visit Edinburgh sometimes at the weekend. Remember, this is an important decision. Try to find a friend or a member of the family who you can talk to.

4 **Language: comparatives**

Look at these sentences:

Exeter is **smaller than** Edinburgh.

Exeter's climate is **better than** Edinburgh's climate.

The course in Exeter **is more interesting than** the course in Edinburgh.

There are two comparative forms.

1. With **short** adjectives, like *small, big, fast, cheap* and *heavy*, we add *~er* to the adjective:

> small**er**, bigg**er**, fast**er**, cheap**er**, heavi**er**

2. With most **long** adjectives (two syllables or more), like *interesting, pleasant* and *comfortable*, we add *more* before the adjective:

> Handwritten letters are **more** interesting than e-mail.

Note: a) Some short adjectives (e.g. *good, bad*) are irregular. They change their form to make the comparative (e.g. *better than, worse than*).

     b) The opposite of *more* is *less:* E-mail is **less** interesting than handwritten letters.

Language: superlatives

Look at these sentences:

Bangkok has **the tallest** hotel in the world. It is 319m, and has 89 storeys.

The best time to visit Korea is in the spring.

The White House is **the most famous** building in Washington.

We use the superlative forms *~est* and *the most* if we are comparing more than two things.

Read through Kate's letter and Aunt Sarah's reply again. Underline examples of comparatives and superlatives. The first two examples in Kate's letter have already been underlined.

 Sam and Yoko are writing about e-mail and letters. Answer these questions:

a. Which does Sam prefer?

b. Which does Yoko prefer?

E-mail or *letters?*

Although e-mail is faster and cheaper, I don't think it's very personal. People write e-mails very quickly, without thinking about the person they are writing to. However, when we write a letter it takes longer and we have more time to think about what we want to say. It's also more interesting to receive a handwritten letter. You see an envelope with your name and address on it and it's exciting, whereas an e-mail seems less personal. You can also put things in the envelope along with the letter, such as photographs or something you have cut out of a newspaper.

It takes so long to write a letter, and then sometimes the letter can take weeks to get to your friend. On the other hand, an e-mail can take just a few minutes to get to the other side of the world. E-mails are also more fun than letters, and writing on a keyboard is easier than writing with a pen. My handwriting, which is really terrible, is very difficult to read. But when I write an e-mail there's no problem. By the way, if you have a digital camera or a scanner, you can also send photographs by e-mail, which is more convenient than sending them in an envelope.

7 Complete the tables for Sam and Yoko that compare e-mail and letters. Put ✓ in the correct boxes.

Sam	E-MAIL	LETTERS
faster		
cheaper		
more interesting		
less personal		

Yoko	E-MAIL	LETTERS
slower		
more fun		
easier		
less convenient		

8 **Language: connecting words**

We use connecting words such as *however, but, on the other hand,* and *whereas* to join ideas. Put a circle around the connecting words in the following sentences:

a. Exeter's winters are not very cold, whereas Edinburgh has cold and windy winters.

b. Edinburgh has cold and windy winters. On the other hand, Exeter's winters are not very cold.

c. Exeter's winters are not very cold, but Edinburgh has cold and windy winters.

d. Edinburgh has cold and windy winters. However, Exeter's winters are not very cold.

Find the following connecting words in Sam's and Yoko's paragraphs. Put a circle around them.

however   but   on the other hand   whereas

9 Complete these sentences in your own words. Use connecting words.

a. Istanbul and Ankara are very different cities. Istanbul is a very old city and is situated on the coast, whereas _____

b. I'd like to visit Germany, but _____

c. My father is trying to decide whether to leave England and go to work in Singapore. On the one hand, Singapore is a beautiful, modern place with good roads and high salaries. On the other hand, _____

d. There's a new shopping mall near my house. However, _____

_____

Sentence building

 Look at the comparative sentences in the table below.

What?	Verb	Adjective + ~er	*than*	What?	.
A keyboard	is	easier to use	than	a pen	.
Edinburgh	has	colder winters	than	Exeter	.
E-mail messages	are	faster	than	letters	.

Now add these sentences to the table. Put the words in the correct order first.

a. London / Rome / has / than / summers / hotter

b. juice / is / fresh / cola / healthier / than / fruit

c. taller / usually / date palms / coconut palms / are / than

d. prepare / an omlette / easier / boiled egg / to / than / is

Look at these comparative sentences. They contain *more* or *less*.

What?	Verb	*more/less*	Adjective	*than*	What?	.
Exeter's climate	is	more	comfortable	than	Edinburgh's climate	.
Videos	are	less	interesting	than	novels	.
E-mail	is	more	reliable	than	ordinary mail	.

Now add these sentences to the table. Put the words in the correct order first.

a. difficult / Chinese / than / English / is / more / learn / to

b. messages / than / letters / E-mail / personal / less / are / handwritten

c. less / an / a / useful / phone / phone / is / ordinary / mobile / than

d. gold / is / silver / expensive / than / more

12 Use these pictures to write comparative sentences. Follow this pattern:

What?	Verb	Adjective + *~er* / *more* + adjective	*than*	What?	.

Example: (wet) *London is wetter than Cairo.*

a. (intelligent) _____

b. (cheap) _____

c. (beautiful) _____

d. (good) _____

e. (quick) _____

Joining ideas

 Language: *who* and *which* clauses – defining and non-defining

Read these sentences. They both contain *which* **clauses**. What is the difference between the two clauses?

a) Moscow State University, which is the largest university in Russia, is situated on a hill overlooking Moscow.

b) The university **which is the most suitable for your needs** is in St. Petersburg.

Clause a) just gives extra information about the university. It is **non-defining**.

Clause b) tells us **exactly** which university the writer is writing about. It is **defining**.

Now look at these sentences. They both contain *who* **clauses**. Underline them. Which is defining and which is non-defining?

c) The people who live next door are from Hong Kong.

d) My neighbour, who is a teacher from Iran, has invited us all to his house tomorrow.

Note: In defining clauses it is possible to put *that* in place of *who* or *which*:

The university **that** is the most suitable for your needs is in St. Petersburg.
The people **that** live next door are from Hong Kong.

Read the letters from Kate and Aunt Sarah on pages 61–62 and the paragraphs about e-mail and letters on page 63.

a. Put a box around any *who* or *which* clauses.

b. How many defining clauses can you find? _____

 Find the defining *who* and *which* clauses in these sentences. Underline them.

a. I managed to find the homework which the teacher had asked me about.

b. On our trip to India last year the place which I liked best was Darjeeling.

c. Yesterday in the supermarket I saw the woman who reads the news on Channel 33.

d. That's the car which I want to buy.

e. 'People who need people are the luckiest people in the world.'

15 **Match these sentences with the defining *which* (or *that*) and *who* (or *that*) clauses. Then write the sentences out in full in your notebook. (Make sure you put the full stops in the right place!)**

a. That's the man.

b. We went to see the film.

c. The car is too expensive.

d. The waitress has disappeared.

e. The country is China.

f. Every year the college presents a prize to the student.

... that gets the best results

... who we gave our order to

... that you recommended

... that I like the best

... which has the largest population in the world

... who stole my bag

 16 **Look at the pictures below. Now complete the sentences with defining *which* (or *that*) and *who* (or *that*) clauses.**

a. That's the driver who/that _____.

b. The computer _____ has broken down.

c. Paris is the city _____.

d. People _____ are known as 'fans' or 'supporters'.

Definitions

 17 **Look at these definitions.**

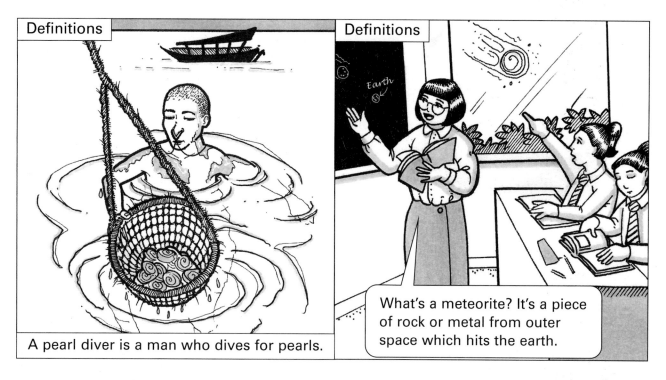

Definitions

A pearl diver is a man who dives for pearls.

Definitions

Earth

What's a meteorite? It's a piece of rock or metal from outer space which hits the earth.

a. Underline the defining clauses in the two definitions.

b. Use your dictionary to write definitions for the following nouns. Use defining *who*, *which* or *that* clauses.

> an answering machine   a taxi-driver
> a pilot   a doctor   a roof-rack

Punctuation

 18 **Language:** commas and clauses

Look at these sentences:

a) Jordan, which is famous for its historical sites, has become very popular with tourists.

b) The historical site which attracts most tourists to Jordan is the ancient city of Petra.

Non-defining clauses (Sentence a) are placed between two commas or between a comma and a full stop. There are no commas before or after a **defining clause** (Sentence b).

Some of these sentences need commas and some do not. Add commas where necessary.

a. Canberra which is the capital of Australia is not the biggest city in the country.

b. The shop had sold out of Jasmine Mystery which is my favourite perfume.

c. The man who robbed the bank was arrested yesterday.

d. The main course was sardines which are popular in Portugal.

e. Last week I wrote a letter to the college that I want to study in.

f. Yu Lin said she wanted to speak to the woman who was in charge of the shop.

g. The programme that I wanted to watch was cancelled at the last minute.

h. Peter who is a well-known journalist writes for a Cape Town newspaper.

i. All appointments have been cancelled by the president who has a slight stomach upset.

Better paragraphs

Connecting words

19 **Complete this passage with the words and phrases in the list.**

> although   when   whereas   however   on the one hand
> who   which   but   less   more

Is life better now, or was life more rewarding in the past? (a)_____ we

have more material things nowadays, such as cars, televisions, videos and so on.

(b)_____ on the other hand, some people think that we were happier in the

past, (c)_____ we had fewer possessions and life was (d)_____ complicated.

My grandfather, for example, was a fisherman. He lived in a small village on the coast

and had a very simple life. There was no electricity and the family had to bring water

from a nearby well, (e)_____ they shared with the whole village. (f)_____,

I have never seen a man as happy as my grandfather.

Life is certainly (g)_____ comfortable nowadays. People (h)_____ live in cities

have air-conditioning, hot and cold water and heating in the winter, (i)_____ in the

old days these things were unheard of. One thing surprises me. (j)_____ we

have all of these comforts at home, many people like to take a tent at the weekends

and go camping in the countryside. Perhaps they are looking for a simpler way of life.

Organization

20 **Put these sentences in the correct order to make two paragraphs. Write the paragraphs in your notebook.**

— for and against

1 **Is nuclear power a good alternative to other sources of power such as oil, gas and hydroelectric power?**

   a. On the other hand, oil and gas can cause a great deal of damage to the environment.

   b. For example, nuclear power is relatively cheap.

   c. Although the cost of building a power plant is high, the running costs are very low.

   d. Nuclear power is also very clean.

   e. There are many points in its favour.

   f. Not only does the process of producing power cause very little pollution, but also there is very little damage to the environment through mining and transporting plutonium.

2 **However, there are many strong arguments against using nuclear power.**

   a. There is also the problem of nuclear waste.

   b. Nuclear power has a poor safety record and there have been many accidents around the world.

   c. For these reasons nuclear power is likely to decline in popularity.

   d. For example, the explosion at a reactor in Chernobyl in the Ukraine caused hundreds, perhaps thousands, of deaths.

   e. The most powerful argument is safety.

   f. Nobody knows how we can get rid of it safely.

Style

 When we think about style we need to think about the reader. Is the reader a general reader, a friend, an official, a teacher or a scientist? We write in different styles for different readers. If you were writing a letter to a friend, the style would probably be informal. You might use contractions (*you're* instead of *you are*) and shortened words (*TV* instead of *television*).

a. Who is the reader of the text about nuclear power? _____

b. Is the style formal or informal? _____

c. Who is the reader of Kate's paragraph on page 61? _____

d. Is the style formal or informal? _____

The following letter is a response to a job advertisement. Choose the more formal option and write the letter out in full in your notebook.

Dear Sir,
I have seen your (a) <u>advert/advertisement</u> for a trainee manager in the *Caribbean Times*. The job sounds (b) <u>very interesting/great</u> and I wonder if you could (c) <u>give me/send me</u> details of the job and an application form.

(d) <u>I'm/I am</u> a student at the International University of Mexico. I will be leaving university in the summer and I (e) <u>would like to find/want to get</u> a job in catering. My first language is Spanish, but I speak and write English (f) <u>OK/quite well</u> and I also know (g) <u>a little/a bit of</u> French.

I have (h) <u>lots/a great deal</u> of experience in catering as I have worked in my uncle's restaurant during the vacations. I also spent two months working in a hotel in Mexico City last summer. It was a (i) <u>really/very</u> useful experience.

(j) <u>I've got/I have</u> some excellent references which I can send if (k) <u>you want/you wish</u>.

(l) <u>Hoping to hear from you./I look forward to hearing from you.</u>

(m) <u>Yours faithfully, /Regards,</u>

Free writing

22 **Francis lives in Manila, in the Philippines. He has a difficult decision to make. Read his letter to a magazine and write a reply. Give him your advice. Begin your letter like this:**
Dear Francis,

Some people think I am in a lucky position. Two companies have offered me jobs. One job is in my uncle's travel company in Manila, the other is with an airline company in Riyadh in Saudi Arabia. The money in Saudi Arabia is much better, and as the company is large the promotion prospects will be better. I have a wife and two children and they can come with me to Riyadh. The children will start primary school in September. On the other hand, I like my uncle very much and the work in his travel company will be interesting. I would have to arrange tours and accommodation for foreign tourists who are visiting the Philippines. Also, I could be near my parents if I stay in Manila. They are very old now and in poor health. However, I have to think about the future of my children too. What is best for them? What shall I do?

23 **A friend is thinking of moving to Australia to work. He/she is planning to go either to Canberra or to Sydney. Write a paragraph for your friend comparing the two cities. Use the information in the table. Add your own ideas and suggestions.**

	Canberra	Sydney
Description	Small modern city, capital of Australia, government the main employer, some light industry and tourism	Largest city in Australia, major port, the main industrial and commercial centre, beautiful harbour and beaches
Location	South East Australia – inland, located on a river in an agricultural area	South East Australia – located on Pacific coast
Climate	Cold and wet winters (sometimes snow) – warm and dry summers	Mild winters and warm summers
Population	Over 300,000	Over 3.5 million

24 Read the paragraphs comparing e-mail and letters on page 63 again. Now write a paragraph in your notebook to compare the telephone with e-mail or letters. Use comparatives and superlatives.

25 Write a paragraph in your notebook to compare the city, town or village you live in with the way it was in the past. How is the place different? Which things are better? Which things are worse? Use comparatives and superlatives.

Use this checklist to edit your writing in Exercises 22–25.

CHECKLIST	Exercise			
	22	23	24	25
How many sentences are there?				
How many full stops (.) are there?				
Does every sentence begin with a capital letter?				
Does every sentence have a verb?				
Have you checked your spelling?				
Can you make your writing **better**?				

Editing

26 Read this paragraph comparing two buildings. It is part of a report for a company that wants to rent a new building for offices. Find 15 mistakes in grammar and spelling. Then write the paragraph out in full in your notebook.

There are two buildings which they are suitabel for the company. One is a building called Panorama House. It located close to the city centre in Station Road. The total area is 1,350sq m. It has six floors and a small reception area. Ther are six toilets and a small kitchen. From the sixth floor there are lovly views of the city. The second possibility is a bilding called Park Mansions, which it is much larger then Panorama House. It has eight floores. The reception area is biger too, wich it is very important for the company. Unfortunately the rent is more expensiver than the rent for Panorama House. It is $ 6,000 per month, wheras the rent for Panorama House is only $ 5,000. The location is less convenient too. Panorama House is more closer to the city centre.

27 Read this paragraph which someone wrote for an encyclopaedia. There are no mistakes but the style is wrong. Write it in a less personal and more formal style in your notebook. The first two examples of bad style are underlined.

Flowering plants

There are <u>lots of</u> different types of plants, <u>like</u> ferns, conifers and angiosperms. The largest group of plants are angiosperms, which we also call flowering plants. Flowering plants produce flowers which produce seeds and fruit. Well, we can divide flowering plants into two more types. We call these monocots and dicots. The monocot, which, by the way, means 'one seed-leaf', has got long narrow leaves. The veins in the leaves all go in the same direction. An example of one of these is the palm tree. On the other hand, the dicot (that's 'two seed-leaf') has got broader leaves.

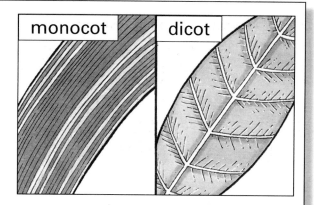

The veins are different too. There's a main vein and then there are little veins branching off. A tomato plant is an example of a dicot. You can see these two kinds of angiosperm in the picture.

Vocabulary building

Regular adjectives

28 Complete this table. Make sure you spell the comparatives and superlatives correctly.

	comparative	superlative
cold	colder	the coldest
hot		the hottest
big		
wet		

	comparative	superlative
nice		
heavy		
dry		
easy		

Irregular adjectives

 29 Complete this table with the correct form.

	good	bad	much/many	little	old
comparative			more		older
superlative	the best			the least	

30 **Complete these facts with superlatives and the names in this list. Use your notebook.**

> Al Azziziyah   Indonesia   Baikal   Antarctica   Nile   Venezuela

a. Lake _____ in Siberia is the world's _____ lake. It is more than 1,600m deep.

b. The _____ river in the world is the _____.

c. _____ is the country with the _____ number of islands. There are more than 13,000.

d. The _____ waterfall in the world is Angel Falls in _____. It is 978m in height.

e. The _____ place on earth is _____. The average temperature is –57.8°C.

f. _____ in Libya is the _____ place on earth. A temperature of 58°C was recorded there.

31 **Look at the questions below. The missing words are all long adjectives found in this unit. Write the answers in the puzzle below and find the vertical word. It is also an adjective.**

a. I think the course at Harvard University is the most _____ for you.
b. This armchair is much more _____ than that wooden chair.
c. The weather is _____ at the moment. It's not too hot and not too cold.
d. I think letters are more _____ than e-mails.
e. That book was very _____. I'd like to read it again.
f. Why don't you learn Spanish. It's less _____ than German.
g. I like my old car, but it's not very _____.
h. The children said that they'd enjoyed *Star Wars*. It was very _____.
i. Einstein was one of the most _____ people who has ever lived.

↓

a. __ __ __ __ __ __ __ __

b. __ __ __ __ __ __ __ __ __ __ __

c. __ __ __ __ __ __ __ __

d. __ __ __ __ __ __ __ __

e. __ __ __ __ __ __ __ __ __ __ __

f. __ __ __ __ __ __ __ __ __

g. __ __ __ __ __ __ __ __

h. __ __ __ __ __ __ __ __

i. __ __ __ __ __ __ __ __ __ __ __ __

Looking at text

1 **Julia is writing about her college. Read the paragraph and complete the graph below. It shows the number of students in the college.**

I have been studying at the New International College in Silver Springs, central Australia, for three years. I am a student in the Science faculty, and I study maths, chemistry and physics. The college, which was built in 1995, is situated in a desert area about 15km from the town. Since it was opened, the college has grown rapidly and now is one of the biggest in Australia. In 1995 there were only 500 students, who came from central Australia, and there were three faculties – Law, Science and Humanities. In 1997 the number of students increased to 3,000 and two new facilities opened, Education and Business. Now the college has more than 12,000 students, who come from many different countries, and the number of faculties has increased to eight. The college has also become more attractive during this time. Because the campus had no trees or gardens in the early days, it used to be very dry and dusty. However, now there are gardens everywhere with fountains, flowers and hundreds of trees. We also have good sports facilities. At the moment the authorities are building a new swimming pool.

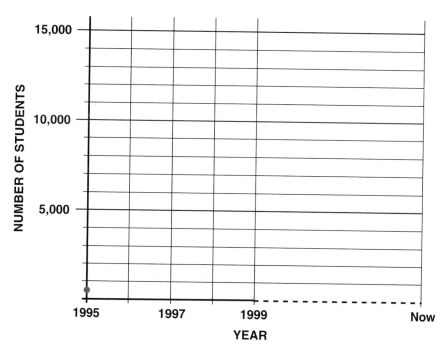

NEW INTERNATIONAL COLLEGE –
Student Numbers

Answer these questions.

a. When was the college opened? _____

b. Where did the first students come from? _____

c. Where do they come from now? _____

d. Why was the campus dry and dusty in the early days?

_____

e. Why is the campus more attractive now? _____

_____

 ## Language: past to present

Underline the verbs in these sentences. Then underline *for* and *since*.

a. Hizo has been studying at the college for six years.

b. The students have been working hard for the past month.

c. Our city has changed a lot since I was a boy.

d. McDuncan's has built five new restaurants since 1998.

When we describe a period which continues from past to present we often use these verb forms:

have/has + ...~ed (*has changed, have studied*, etc.)

have/has + been + ...~ing (*has been studying, have been working*, etc.)

We often use these verbs with **for** (*for six months, for ten minutes, for ages*) and **since** (*since 1999, since Tuesday, since I was little*).

Look at Julia's paragraph again.

a. Find *past to present* verbs in Julia's paragraph and underline them.

   How many are there? _____

b. Find a clause beginning with *since* and underline it.

c. Underline *which* and *who* clauses. How many are there? _____

d. Find the phrase *used to be* and underline it.

e. Complete this sentence with your own words:

   When I was little I used to _____

4 **Read this paragraph about computers.**

C · O · M · P · U · T · E · R · S

Fifty years ago computers were so big that they filled a room. Nowadays <u>they</u> are placed on desks, carried in the pocket or even fitted into tiny instruments such as watches. They have been getting smaller and smaller because of improved technology. They have also been getting cheaper, which means that more people are able to own <u>one</u>. At the same time computers have also been getting more powerful. The first computers could do just a few calculations in a second, whereas a modern microcomputer can do millions // in a second. The first computer // able to store a programme, was built at Manchester University in 1948. This was a huge 'mainframe' computer. In 1960 the tiny silicon chip was invented, and because of <u>this</u> it became possible to build much smaller and faster computers. In 1981 IBM introduced the first desktop microcomputer, the PC (personal computer). Since <u>then</u> sales // have risen dramatically. Almost every office desk now has its own PC, which is the most widely-used type of computer in the world.

a. Put these inventions in the correct order.

___ the silicon chip   ___ the desktop PC   ___ the mainframe computer

b. Complete this sentence:

For the last fifty years computers have been getting _____, _____

and more _____.

5 **Look at the paragraph about computers again.**

a. What do the underlined words refer to?

they _____   one _____

this _____   then _____

b. Look for this symbol // in the paragraph above. Decide where to add the following words.

> which was   of computers   of calculations

6   **Read about coffee production in Palania and complete the graph.**

The graph shows coffee production in Palania from 1985 up to the present day. During this period production levels have fluctuated greatly. In 1985 the total was 100,000 tonnes. This total increased steadily and reached a total of 150,000 tonnes in 1990. In 1991, however, there was a severe hurricane in the region, which destroyed many of the trees. Because of this, coffee production fell sharply that year to 120,000 tonnes. The following year production went up again, and by 1995 it reached 180,000 tonnes. However, in 1996 there was a collapse in the world coffee price. Too many countries were producing too much coffee and this caused the price to fall. As a result, many of the trees had to be destroyed in order to stop over-production of coffee. Production dropped to just under 100,000 tonnes in 1996 and remained at that level for the next two years. For the last few years, however, production has been increasing rapidly and the present total is just over 200,000 tonnes. The prospects for coffee production in the future are very good.

COFFEE PRODUCTION
In Palania

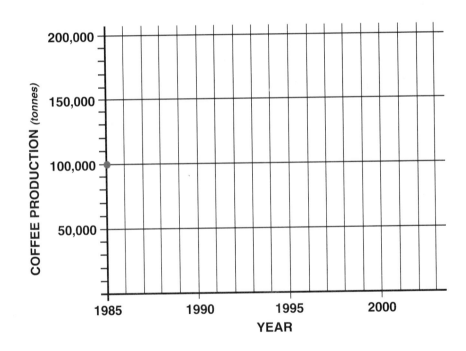

7   **Language: time**

1) A point of time in the past
   (past simple)

2) A period in the past, now finished
   (past continuous)

3) A period starting in the past and continuing till now *(present perfect/ present perfect continuous)*

Present

Match the time diagrams with these six sentences.

a. Since 1981 sales of computers have risen dramatically. ___

b. Computers have been getting smaller and smaller. ___

c. In 1991 there was a severe hurricane in the region. ___

d. The campus has become more attractive during this time. ___

e. Too many countries were producing too much coffee throughout 1996. ___

f. This total increased steadily and reached a total of 150,000 tonnes in 1990. ___

Read about coffee production again. Find examples of time types 1–3 and write them below.

1) _____

2) _____

3) _____

Sentence building

 Put these words in the correct order. Then write the sentences in the table. They all describe past to present time.

a. since / bank / Felix / working / has / a / in / 1999 / been

b. six o'clock / washing / their / have / the boys / car / been / since

c. girl / Sarah / little / she / a / since / known / I / was / have

d. many / family / kept / for / horses / have / years / my

e. has / minutes / bus / for / for / a / twenty / Andy / waiting / been

f. centuries / grown / the valley / people / rice / for / have / in

Who?/What?	Verb	What?/Where?/How?	*since* + When	.
Carlos	has been studying	at the college	since last year	.
Coffee production	has gone down	rapidly	since the hurricane destroyed so many trees	.
				.

81

Who?/What?	Verb	What?/Where?/How?	*for* + How long	.
Maria	has been working	at United Cosmetics	for six months	.
Fatima and her family	have lived	in Casablanca	for two years	.

9 Write sentences like those in Exercise 8. Write two with *since* and two with *for*.

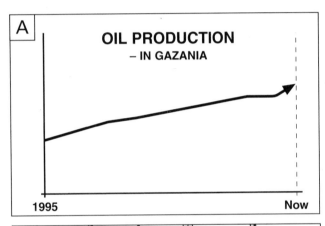

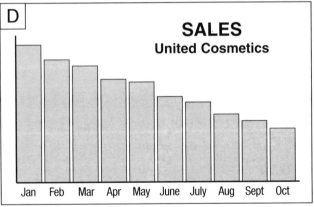

a. *Oil production* _____

b. *We* _____

c. *Annie* _____

d. *Sales* _____

10 Write four sentences in your notebook about yourself or people you know. Use *past to present* verbs with *for* and *since*.

Joining ideas

Language: *because* clauses

A *because* clause tells us **why** something happened. It can come at the beginning or the end of a sentence.

First part of the sentence	*Because* clause
The campus was dry and dusty in the early days	because it had no trees or gardens.

Because clause	Last part of the sentence
Because it had no trees or gardens,	the campus was dry and dusty in the early days.

Match these sentences. Then join each pair to make one sentence and write the sentences in your notebook. Use *because*.

1) Keiko is studying business studies, English and computing.

2) Coffee production fell dramatically last year.

3) More and more people are buying computers.

4) Nina couldn't come to the birthday party yesterday.

5) The government is building ten new schools.

6) Boris has been trying to save money for the last six months.

a. They are becoming cheaper and cheaper.

b. She was taking an examination at the college.

c. He wants to go on holiday to San Francisco in the summer.

d. Many trees were destroyed by bad weather.

e. The population of the country has been increasing rapidly in recent years.

f. She wants to work for a large multinational company.

 Complete these sentences with *because* clauses. Write the sentences out in full in your notebook.

a. The road through the mountains has been closed for two days ...

b. Elena got excellent marks in the examination ...

c. Ali couldn't watch the film on television yesterday ...

d. Hari has been working very hard since the beginning of the year ...

e. The price of bananas has gone up recently ...

Language: *because of this/as a result*

We can also use the connectors **because of this** and **as a result** to link two sentences:

Paulo left the gate open when he went out.

The sheep ate all his vegetable.

Paulo left the gate open when he went out. **Because of this,** the sheep ate all of his vegetables.

Paulo left the gate open when he went out. **As a result,** the sheep ate all of his vegetables.

Read the paragraph about coffee production on page 80 again. Find two sentences beginning with *because of this* and *as a result*. Write them in your notebook.

Clauses

In the table below are some of the clauses we have studied in *Better Writing*. Add these parts of sentences to the table.

a. we decided to cancel the trip to Star Island.

b. the juice is extracted from the fruit.

c. we decided to make the trip to Star Island.

d. many new trees had to be planted.

e. you can make a phone call from anywhere.

f. there were only 500 students and three faculties.

Clause	Last part of the sentence
When the college opened,	
As the machine spins around,	
In order to increase coffee production,	
If you have got a mobile phone,	
Although the weather was bad,	
Because the weather was bad,	

Remember *who* and *which* clauses? Look at the *who* and *which* clauses in these two sentences. They are non-defining (they just give extra information).

> *The college, which was built in 1995, is situated in a desert area about 15km from the city.*
>
> *Now the college has more than 12,000 students,* **who come from many different countries.**

Complete these sentences with *who* or *which* clauses.

a. The mathematics teacher, who _____, has been teaching

   at the college since 1995.

b. The Giza pyramids, which _____, are popular with tourists

   from all over the world.

c. Nelson Mandela, who _____, retired in 1999.

d. I received a letter from a friend of mine called Mike, who _____

   _____.

e. Last summer my family visited Istanbul, which _____.

f. Hummus, which _____, is quite easy to prepare.

16 ▶ Language: reduced clauses

Look at the sentences below. They all contain **defining clauses**.

The car **which is parked near the tree** belongs to my cousin.

The car **parked near the tree** belongs to my cousin.

The words ***which is*** are omitted in the second sentence. There is no difference in meaning.

Now look at this pair of sentences:

The man **who is in charge of the factory** is called Peter Yu.

The man **in charge of the factory** is called Peter Yu.

The words ***who is*** are omitted in the second sentence. There is no difference in meaning.

Reduce these defining clauses. Write the sentences out in full in your notebook.

a. The first computer which was able to store a program was built at Manchester University in 1948.

b. The man who is wearing a brown jacket is a chemistry professor.

c. The tall tower that is built like a rocket is the Holiday Hotel.

d. The president is the short, fat man who is speaking to the old lady.

e. The country that is most famous for growing coffee is Brazil.

f. Andrea Bocelli is a blind Italian singer who is known for his wonderful voice.

Punctuation

 17 **Rewrite this paragraph about changes in aeroplanes. Add capital letters, full stops and commas where necessary. Then write the paragraph out in full in your notebook.**

aeroplanes have been getting bigger and faster over the years the first modern aeroplane was the boeing 247 which was introduced in 1933 it had room for 10 passengers during the second world war the jet engine was developed the first jet airliner which was called the comet started service in 1952 it had four jet engines and could fly at 885kph later in 1958 pan american airlines introduced the boeing 707 which could carry 112 passengers because of the powerful engines the plane was able to cross the atlantic from new york to london in less than eight hours which was half the time of the old propeller aircraft

Better paragraphs

Style

 18 **Read Sarah's letter on page 87.**

a. Add the clauses from the list below. Then write the letter out in full in your notebook.

1) if I needed help

2) who is a friend of my father's

3) because I was late for class

4) if it's not too hot

5) which has been rather boring

6) which is just outside my bedroom window

7) who's not working at the moment

8) As I was running down the stairs from the first floor to the ground floor

b. What style do you think the letter is in? Why do you think so? Find three things that are typical of that style.

Dear Elena,

I'm writing this letter to you from my bed. I broke my leg badly three weeks ago on the stairs in the college. I was in a hurry. I slipped and fell to the bottom. I felt a terrible pain in my left leg and I couldn't move. At the hospital the doctor told me that my leg was broken. After resetting my leg in plaster, he said that I should rest at home for at least a month and then come back to see him. He told me to phone him. Since then I've been at home. I've been getting better bit by bit. I've been reading books and magazines and watching TV, but I can't wait until I can walk again. Sometimes I sit in the garden. My older sister has been looking after me. She's been wonderful!

Please write and let me know your news!

Best wishes,

Sarah

Organization

 Put these sentences in the correct order (the first and last sentences are already in position). Then write the paragraph out in full in your notebook.

1. **In 1985 the amount of raw sugar produced in Azaria was 6.5 million tonnes.**

   a. Then, in 1995, there was a very poor sugar harvest due to very dry conditions all through the year.

   b. Since then there has been plenty of rainfall every year but production has not risen greatly.

   c. It remained at this low level for the next three years as the war continued.

   d. This total made the country one of the largest producers of sugar in the world.

   e. Farm workers were needed in the army and as a result sugar production fell sharply to less than 3 million tonnes.

   f. However, at the end of the war, in 1989, production started to improve steadily.

   g. It reached 5.5 million tonnes in 1992 and stayed at this high level for the next two years.

   h. Crops in many areas died because of a lack of water and as a result production fell to just under 4 million tonnes.

   i. However, in the following year, 1986, a war began with the Pandoran Republic.

11. **It has been fluctuating around the 4.5 million tonnes level.**

Connecting words

20 **Read this passage about shopping. Add these connecting words and phrases:**

> however   also   since   although   because   which
> because of this   whereas   which   but

In the past shopping was a social occasion. People used to go to their local market not only to buy food and other goods, (a)_____ also to find out what was going on in their community. Each shop or market stall sold a particular product – fruit, vegetables, meat, perfumes, soap, cloth, etc. (b)_____ a shopping trip took a long time. People went from shop to shop chatting with the shopkeeper and discussing everything from prices to politics.

(c)_____, in the 1950s and 1960s there were great changes in the lifestyles of many people. More and more people had a refrigerator, (d)_____ meant it was possible to store fresh food at home. More and more people were (e)_____ able to afford cars. (f)_____ then shops have increased in size and have become more and more centralized. (g)_____ in the past we bought things from many different shopkeepers, we now shop in large department stores, supermarkets and shopping malls, (h)_____ sell everything under one roof. We no longer have to worry about the weather. People drive to these centres and load up their cars with goods. (i)_____ people have refrigerators and freezers, they can buy all the food they need for weeks. (j)_____ shopping has become easier and more pleasant, it has also become less personal. It is now possible to buy everything you need in a supermarket or department store without chatting to anyone.

Free writing

21 Describe the place where you are studying. When was it opened? How many students were there when it first opened? How many students are there now? What other changes are there? What other changes have there been?

22 Look at this graph. It shows coffee production in South Abelia since 1990. Write a paragraph in your notebook to describe the graph.

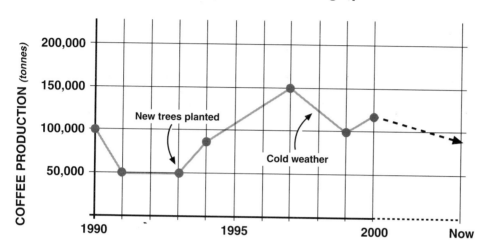

23 Read the passage about computers on page 79 again. Now look at this information about the changes in cars since 1907. Write a paragraph in your notebook to describe the changes.

Cars	
1907	First cheap car – the Model T
1938	Volkswagen Beetle – very popular
1950s	Bigger and bigger cars (e.g. Cadillac)
1970s	Increase in fuel costs
Since 1970s	Smaller, more economical cars
Now	400 million in the world Cars are more comfortable, faster, safer and more economical

24 Write a letter to a friend. Describe something that has happened to you recently. Describe the changes it has made to your life. (For example you have a new job, you have moved to a new house or flat, you have started a new course of study, etc.) Use your notebook.

Use this checklist to edit your writing in Exercises 21–24.

CHECKLIST	Exercise 21	22	23	24
How many sentences are there?				
How many full stops (.) are there?				
Does every sentence begin with a capital letter?				
Does every sentence have a verb?				
Have you checked your spelling?				
Can you make your writing **better**?				

Editing

 25 **Read this paragraph about global warming. It is part of an essay.**

a. Correct spelling and grammatical mistakes. There are 12 mistakes.

b. Make the paragraph **easier to read**. Use connectors and clauses to join the ideas.
   Write the paragraph out in full in your notebook.

Global warming is caused by an increse in the amount of carbon dioxide in the Earth's atmosphere. Carbon dioxide are produced naturally by vegetation. It is important part of the atmosphere. It traps the sun's heat. It warms the surface of the Earth. Normally there is a balance between the gases in the atmospher. In recent years the amount of carbon dioxide has went up. This is becuase of the burning of fossil fuels and the destruction of forests. The temperature of the Earth's surface have been going up. These has meant changes in Earth's climate. Many parts of the world are becoming hoter and drier. Other parts are experiencing more storms and rainfall. Sea level it has also been riasing. This is because the polar ice-caps have been melting.

Vocabulary building

Describing change

26 Divide these verbs into two groups: verbs which mean the same as *increase*, and verbs which mean the same as *decrease*. Write them in the lists below.

> go down   go up   fall   grow   improve   collapse   rise   drop

increase

_____

_____

_____

_____

decrease

_____

_____

_____

_____

Faculties and subjects

27 Find the names of these subjects.

a. C _ _ _ _ _ _ R Y

b. P _ _ _ _ _ S

c. _ I O _ _ _ _ _

d. H _ _ _ O _ _

e. _ _ _ G R _ _ _ _

f. M _ _ _ _ M _ _ _ _ S

g. C _ _ P _ _ _ _ S C _ _ _ _ _

Add other subjects to the list.

_____

28 Find the names of these faculties.

a. S _ _ _ _ _ _

b. L _ _

c. E D _ _ _ _ _ _ _ _

d. A _ _ S

e. E N _ _ _ _ _ _ _ _ G

Add other faculties to the list.

_____

29 **Use these clues to complete the crossword below.**

ACROSS

1. Aeroplanes have been ___ bigger and faster. (7 letters)

5. Sarah has to rest ___ her broken leg is better. (5)

7. In the past people shopped in markets. ___ many people shop in department stores and supermarkets. (8)

11. Supermarkets are very convenient for shoppers. ___ the other hand, they are less personal than markets. (2)

12. The way out of a room or building is the ___. (4)

13. After picking, dates are ___ in the sun. (5)

16. Jericho, ___ is the oldest city in the world, is situated in the Jordan valley. (5)

18. What will happen to the price of oil next year? Will it rise ___ will it fall? (2)

19. My cousin has been in secondary school ___ two years. (3)

20. I've been ___ to save money since the beginning of the semester. (6)

22. The university authorities ___ building a new library on the campus. (3)

24. Computers have become smaller and more powerful. They have ___ become cheaper. (4).

26. The Lucky Star Hotel, which has been ___ for three months, is going to open again on Saturday. (6)

28. The population is rising rapidly. ___ a result, several more schools will be needed in the future. (2)

29. Because there were ___ trees or gardens, the campus was very dusty. (2)

30. 'Are you going to feed the sheep?' 'No, I ___ them half an hour ago.' (3)

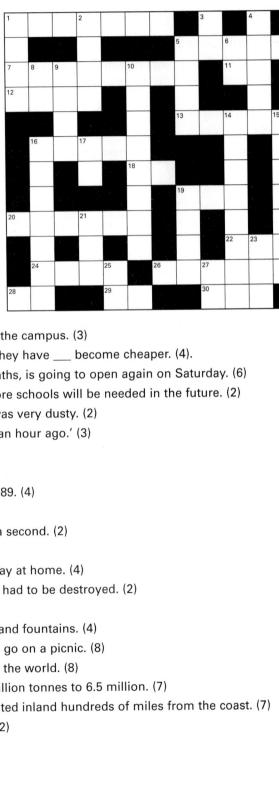

DOWN

1. Production of raw sugar has ___ down steadily since 1989. (4)

2. Is that the dress ___ you want to buy? (4)

3. Modern computers can do millions of calculations ___ a second. (2)

4. Sarah has been feeling bored ___ she broke her leg. (5)

5. We ___ to go to the coast every summer but now we stay at home. (4)

6. In order ___ stop over-production of coffee, many trees had to be destroyed. (2)

8. ___ is another name for a cow or bull. (2)

9. The campus is very attractive, ___ many trees, flowers and fountains. (4)

10. ___ the weather forecast was rather bad, we decided to go on a picnic. (8)

14. If global warming continues, sea levels will ___ all over the world. (8)

15. From 1996–1999 the production of coffee ___ from 8 million tonnes to 6.5 million. (7)

16. Bombay is a port on the Indian Ocean, ___ Delhi is located inland hundreds of miles from the coast. (7)

17. Since ___ was opened, the college has grown rapidly. (2)

19. Sarah ___ down some stairs and broke her leg. (4)

21. Almost every office desk has ___ own PC. (3)

23. This colour means 'danger'. (3)

25. Last summer we went ___ holiday to Sweden. (2)

27. Tokyo is one ___ the biggest cities in the world. (2)

To the teacher

While *Better Writing* includes a lot of work at the sentence level, the main focus is on the paragraph. Students move on from accuracy to writing fluency, and from mechanical skills (capitalization, spelling, punctuation) to the skills required to write longer stretches of text. The aim is make students aware of what 'better' writing involves: that is, writing which is more cohesive, better organized, more appropriate to the reader and easier to read – as well as writing which is more accurate.

How is grammar approached?

Though this book is not a grammar course, items of grammar are dealt with where appropriate. The range of grammatical structures used includes the present passive, reported speech forms and the present and past perfect tenses. Grammatical terminology is kept to a minimum. The structure of a sentence is explained as far as possible through a simplified teaching grammar, using terms such as *Who? How? Which? What?* and *When?* Students are, however, expected to be familiar with basic grammatical terms such as *adjective, noun, verb, clause, passive* and *past participle*.

What is the sequence through a unit?

Each unit follows a similar format, starting from a *Looking at text* section focusing on how specific language items are being used in context, through to a *Free writing* section towards the end of the unit, where students produce their own paragraphs. In between, there are a number of activities where students are asked to manipulate language, rearrange sentences, or complete guided paragraphs.

The main steps followed through each unit are:

Looking at text: This section contains a number of reading texts which illustrate the functional area of the unit and serve as a model for later free writing. The activities based on the texts are designed to raise the student's awareness of features within them, whether language structures or organizational and cohesive features.

Sentence building: Tables are used to make the structure of sentences clear. Students are asked to reorder words in sentences and to complete tables.

Joining ideas: Here the focus is mainly on the use of clauses to join ideas and shorter sentences in order to produce more cohesive writing.

Punctuation: Exercises in this section focus on the use of capital letters, commas, full stops, speech marks, apostrophes, etc.

Better Paragraphs: Guided activities focus on the organization and cohesion of paragraphs.

Free Writing: In this section students use the paragraphs in *Looking at text* as models to write their own texts. Notes, diagrams and pictures are used to give students guidance.

Editing: Students develop the habit of checking their written work through editing exercises which focus not only on spelling, grammar and punctuation, but also on how clauses and connectors can be used to improve writing.

Build your vocabulary: A variety of activities are used to review the vocabulary areas of the unit. Students improve their vocabulary-learning techniques by a) organizing words into content areas, b) using illustrations to facilitate learning and c) learning collocations of new words.

How should the course be taught?

This depends on the students and teacher. Four different approaches are possible:

1. *Teacher led:* The class is kept at roughly the same point in the course. The teacher introduces each section of the unit and checks progress.

2. *Group work:* In a multi-level class students can be divided into small groups according to writing ability. Groups work through the units together. The teacher can then give greater attention to weaker students.

3. *Individual work:* Students work through the book at their own pace. The teacher monitors progress and checks work during the lesson. However, it is recommended that this approach is adopted only when students are familiar with the structure of the units.

4. *A combination of the above methods*

Should students write in the book?

Gap-fill exercises can be completed in the book if this is acceptable, but for the sake of clarity and encouraging good writing habits, sentence and paragraph writing should be done in notebooks or, where available, on the computer. Writing can also be produced on single sheets or posters for wall displays on themes such as *How things work, How things are made* or *Comparison* (of cities, countries etc.).

Answer key

Unit One

2. b) 's = has, 've = have

4. wide–width, high–height, thick–thickness

5. a) D   b) consists of   c) are white, are blue
c) is, is small   d) are used for

6. a) Our boat has got a small engine at the back.
b) My CD player has got two speakers at the sides.
c) These shirts have got two pockets at the front.

7. a) The Japanese flag has got a red circle in the middle.   b) The camera (This camera) has got a viewfinder on the top.   c) The buses (These buses) have got advertisements on the side.

8. a) There is a red circle in the middle of the Japanese flag.   b) There is a viewfinder on the top of the camera.   c) There are advertisements on the side of the buses.

9. a) A credit card is made of plastic. It is used for paying for goods and services.   b) A knife is made of metal. It is used for cutting things.
c) Envelopes are made of paper. They are used for sending letters.   d) Tyres are made of rubber. They are used for covering wheels.

10. a) The jeep is new with tinted windows and power steering.   b) The watch is oval with silver hands and a gold strap.   c) The phone is small with large, luminous numbers.   d) The boat is green with a white mast and a red sail.

12. I – use – the phone – when I <u>go</u> shopping.
My brother – uses – the car – when he <u>goes</u> camping in the desert.

14. a) When visitors come to Kuwait, – they should take a trip to Kuwait Towers.   b) When you go up in the lift, – you can see the whole of Kuwait.

15. <u>I</u>t's got a memory, but it hasn't got a brain. <u>I</u>t's rectangular in shape and quite thin. <u>I</u>t looks like a briefcase and is about the same size. <u>I</u>t's very easy to carry as it is made mostly of plastic and only weighs about 5kg. <u>W</u>hen you open the lid, you find a screen and a keyboard inside. <u>P</u>eople use these machines when they are travelling. <u>W</u>hat is it?

a) 7 sentences   b) laptop computer

17. a) and   b) with   c) It   d) when   e) There   f) so
g) got   h) also   i) when   j) it

18. a) horse   b) made   c) rectangular   d) long
e) wide   f) thickness   g) height   h) weighs
i) There   j) got   k) shield

23. It <u>has</u> got four legs, but it can't walk. It <u>is</u> rectangular in shape and there is a leg at each corner. It measure<u>s</u> about a metre in <u>height</u>. The top is 1.8m long and 70cm <u>wide</u> and has a thickness <u>of</u> 4cm. Ours is made of wood, but sometimes they are made of plastic or <u>glass</u>. In our house we keep it in the dining <u>r</u>oom.

It's a table.

24. *Suggested answer:*
My friend Yi has got a new radio. He bought it a few days ago. It is black with a red handle. Yi likes the radio very much. It is very light and so he can take it everywhere. He takes the radio with him when he has a shower. (When he has a shower, he takes the radio with him.)

25. not very big, quite big, big, very big

26. a) black   b) white   c) blue   d) red   e) yellow
f) green   g) pink

29. not very good, quite good, good, very good

30.

Unit Two

3. d) this = a base station, there = the telephone exchange

6. The verbs are: a) switch on   b) leave   c) press

7. a) Passive verbs: is made, is guaranteed, must be washed, should be peeled and cut, is switched on, are pushed, is separated, is collected

b) 1 – E (washed),   2 – A (peeled),   3 – D (cut),
4 – B (switched on),   5 – F (pushed),
6 – C (collected)

8. c) remove the lid, clean out the container, remove the jug, pour the juice

9. a) Two R6 batteries – are inserted – into the compartment.   b) A CD – is placed – on the CD tray.   c) The lid – must be closed – firmly.
d) Headphones – are fitted – to the front of the CD player.   e) The headphones – are placed – over the ears.   f) The 'play' button – is pressed.
g) The volume – can be adjusted – as required.

10. a) Insert two R6 batteries into the compartment. b) Place a CD on the CD tray. c) Close the lid firmly. d) Fit the headphones to the front of the CD player. e) Place the headphones over the ears. f) Press the 'play' button. g) Adjust the volume as required.

11. a) Singapore is linked to Malaysia by a causeway. b) Trees and bushes are planted along the sides of the road. c) The fax machine is connected to a telephone point. d) The garage door is opened by a remote control unit.

12. a) The vegetables are peeled and cut into small pieces. b) The signal is sent to an aerial and then transmitted to a telephone exchange. c) The phone is made of plastic and the case made of leather. d The outgoing message is recorded and the machine switched on.

15. *Possible answers:*
a) enter the bank b) leave the house c) have any difficulties with their bookings d) board the bus e) feel ill

17. a) The books belong to **one** student. b) The books belong to **more than one** student. c) The secretary **is** ill. d) The secretary **has** got a fever.

18. a) The dog's got some bad cuts on its leg. b) I'm afraid the radio's broken. c) No change. d) It's situated at the top of a hill. e) There's a flag at the top of the building. f) No change. g) The machine's switched off at the moment. h) Five teachers have their desks in this room. It's called the teachers' room.

19. a) If the caller is in an underground car park, it may be impossible to use the mobile phone.
b) When the tape is full, no further messages can be recorded on the answering machine.
c) In order to avoid damage to the machine, stones must be removed from fruit.
d) Contact your local dealer if you have problems with your new television.
e) As the door closes, the light inside the refrigerator goes off.
f) In order to keep a compact disc in good condition, it should be kept in its cover.
g) When someone leaves a message on the answering machine, a number appears in the display panel.
h) The juice is separated from the pulp as the fruit is pushed into the feed tube.

20. (1) As air is drawn into the drier, it passes over the electric heater. (2) First of all, in order to avoid electrocution, make sure your hands are dry. (3) As you move the drier over your hair, use your styling brush to style your hair. (4) Finally, when your hair is dry, switch the machine off.

21. a) is used for b) consists of c) and so d) are reflected e) If f) is placed g) begins h) In order to i) must be turned j) When k) avoid

22. *Suggested order:*
2–f, 3–g, 4–b, 5–h, 6–d, 7–a, 8–i, 9–c, 10–e.

26. **W**ater-wheels are a very old form of water power. They can be **made** of wood or metal. They are found in many **countries** of the world. For example, the city of Hama in **S**yria is famous for its 17 wooden water-wheels. Water-wheels are usually located on fast-flowing **rivers** or streams. **A**s the river flows, the wheel is turned by the power of the water. The power is used to take **water** from the river for farming.

27. A computer (**it**) is a very powerful instrument. Some computers are heavy and **are** placed on desks. Other computers are quite small and can **be** carried in the pocket. A computer **has** many different uses. Information **is** given to the computer and a set of instructions, called a programme. The computer is **told** what to do by the programme. A computer (**is**) consists of a monitor with a screen, a keyboard, a disk drive, speakers and a mouse. The keyboard and the mouse are **used** for getting information into the computer. The 'output' (**it**) is shown on **a** computer screen.

30. b) aerial c) must d) cellular e) lens f) collected g) pulp h) adjust

vertical word = Damascus

Unit Three

1. 1 – E (soaked) 2 – F (drained) 3 – B (steamed) 4 – D (mixed) 5 – C (poured) 6 – A (served)

7. a) Hummus – is made – by mixing chickpeas and sesame-seed paste together.
b) A message – is recorded – by speaking into the microphone.
c) Drivers – are protected – by wearing their seat-belts.

8. a) boiling in a pan of water. b) throwing the dice. c) pressing a button. d) mixing yellow and blue.

9. *Also* comes after verbs like *is* and *can*. It comes before the main verb.

a) They are also found in other parts of the world. b) They also grow naturally in the Amazon region of Brazil. c) It can also be moved by clicking the mouse. d) She also sings popular music.

11. a) Tehran, which is the capital of Iran, is located in the centre of the country. b) *Satay* is a simple and delicious dish, which is popular throughout South East Asia.

13. There are two possible ways of joining each pair of sentences, as is shown in a):

a) Indonesia, which consists of nearly 14,000 islands, has a population of more than 200 million people. OR Indonesia, which has a population of more than 200 million people, consists of nearly 14,000 islands.   b) Rubber, which needs a hot, humid climate, is grown in tropical countries such as Malaysia.   c) The Panama canal, which connects the Pacific and Atlantic Oceans, is just over 64km long.   d) A fax machine, which works by sending printed material through telephone lines, is an important part of a modern office.   e) The *erhu*, which is a Chinese instrument rather like a Western violin, has only two strings.

14. a) An answering machine records messages, which can then be played back when you get home.
b) My brother has just bought a Nissan Patrol, which is one of the most popular four-wheel-drive vehicles in the world.   c) Last week we visited Petra, which is the most famous historical site in Jordan.   d) The surface of the road is then sprayed with asphalt, which is a dark, sticky substance produced from petroleum.   e) Strips of rubber are passed through rollers, which flatten the strips and produce thin sheets.

16. a) Although fishermen have the money to buy modern boats, they often prefer to use the old wooden ones.   b) Although the car is eight years old, it is in excellent condition.   c) Although Egypt has very low rainfall, many crops can be grown using irrigation.   d) Although the computer is quite powerful, the modem is rather slow.
e) Although it can be very cold in Hong Kong in the winter, it never snows.   f) Although those watches are very cheap, they are also very attractive.   g) Although some perfumes are made in India, most are imported from France.

18. a) **A**lthough the suitcase is very large, it only weighs 6kg.   b) **M**y new cassette player's got two tape decks, which is very useful for copying tapes.
c) **B**uenos **A**ires, which is the capital of **A**rgentina, is situated on the **R**iver **P**late.   d) **Y**oko sends e-mail messages all the time, although she found computers difficult to use at first.   e) **L**ast summer we flew to **S**ingapore on **Q**antas, which is an **A**ustralian airline.   f) **A**lthough **T**oyota is a **J**apanese company, **T**oyota cars are built in many different countries.   g) **T**he carnival in **R**io, which takes place in **F**ebruary every year, attracts thousands of visitors from all over the world.
h) **A** juice extractor can be used for most types of fruit and vegetables, although it is not very suitable for oranges and lemons.

19. a) (1) First of all,   (2) also   (3) Next,
    (4) then   (5) Meanwhile,   (6) Finally,
    b) After 'blinis', ...'   c) After 'caviar' at the end.

20. a) which   b) Although   c) As   d) When
    e) in order to   f) If   g) which   h) until

21. The population of many areas of the world is growing rapidly. As a result there is a great need for new towns; one example is Shatin in the Hong Kong region of China. The new towns are usually built in rural areas. Before building can begin, the land is mapped by surveyors. Aerial and satellite photos are also needed. Then architects, planners and engineers look at the maps, and plans are drawn up for the new town. When everyone has agreed on the plans, work can begin. First of all roads are laid. Electric power and water are brought to the site and drains are dug. Then buildings, such as houses, apartment blocks, schools and shops are constructed. Finally, trees and gardens are planted to make the town more attractive.

25. Cotton is **grown** in hot areas such as Egypt and parts of China. It needs plenty of water, either from
rainfall or from irrigation, and good, rich soils. When the cotton **is** ready, it must **be** harvested quickly before rain can damage it. The cotton **is** sometimes picked by hand, but usually it is picked by machines. The cotton is **collected** and placed in machines, where the fibres (called 'lint') are **separated** from the cotton seeds. The lint is then packed into bales and **sent** to factories where cotton cloth **is** manufactured.

26. **WELCOME** TO PARADISE!

Do you like delicious, spicy food **served** in beautiful surroundings? Yes? Then visit our new 'Paradise Restaurant'. We are **located** in Ocean Avenue in the centre of the city. Our restaurant, which has wonderful views of the city, is on the **tenth** floor of the Toyota Tower. The menu, **which** is prepared by our experienced chef, contains Chinese, Malaysian and Indonesian dishes. Although our prices are low, you will find that the quality of the food is very **high**. Come and visit us soon!

27.

	a bridge	a well	the foundations	a plan	a hole	an omelette
build	✓	✓	✓	✗	✗	✗
draw up	✗	✗	✗	✓	✗	✗
lay	✗	✗	✓	✗	✗	✗
construct	✓	✓	✓	✓	✗	✗
make	✓	✓	✓	✓	✓	✓
drill	✗	✓	✗	✗	✓	✗
dig	✗	✓	✓	✗	✓	✗

28. A) boil   B) drain   C) cover   D) steam   E) measure
    F) heat   G) mix   H) pour   I) add

29. A) cut   B) collect   C) spray   D) pour into   E) plant
    F) transport   G) pick   H) export   I) pass through

30. a) cut   b) made   c) dug   d) laid   e) built   f) sent
    g) taken   h) drawn   i) seen   j) found

Unit Four

1. Picture b

3. a) Regular: asked, replied, lifted, opened, looked, used, explained
   Irregular: went, were, was, told, said, forgot
   b) was beginning

6. a) told   b) explained   c) replied   d) said

7. Picture 1: 'The engine's on fire!'
   Picture 2: 'We are going to land in the sea.'
   Picture 3: 'Put on your life jackets.'

8. a) many = many of the passengers
   some = some of the passengers
   b) he = the pilot, us = the passengers
   c) there = the emergency exit
   d) their = International Air's

10. a) Janet said that she was not feeling well.   b) Our teacher told us that the examinations would be on May 23rd.   c) The man said that he had lost his passport. (The man told the immigration officer that he had lost his passport.)   d) Sam said that he had been there last week.

11. a) The doctor – asked me – if – I was feeling better.
    b) Aziz – asked me – when – I had my lunch break.
    c) Pierre – asked me – if – I spoke French.
    d) The waiter – asked me – what – I wanted to drink.

12. a) After having a large lunch, John fell asleep for twenty minutes.   b) Before starting the boat, make sure you check that there is enough petrol.   c) After living in Rome for six years, we moved to Istanbul.   d) Before buying the dress, Nina tried it on.   e) After writing the letter, Mike faxed it to the head office in Cairo.   f) Before travelling to China, Ibn Batuta visited Mecca.

13. a) Ronaldo, who is an excellent football player, scored six goals last week.   b) I've just had a phone call from my sister, who is studying at a college in Manila.   c) The mechanic, who was very experienced, said he could repair the car by the following day.   d) This morning I went to see the doctor, who said I should rest for three days.   e) Mohsin is reading a book about Atatürk, who was the founder of modern Turkey.   f) Our English teacher, who is very kind, hard-working and helpful, is probably the best teacher in the college.

15. a) The Pathans, who come from the mountainous regions of Pakistan, speak Pashto as their mother tongue.   b) Anna, who has just graduated from the University of Singapore, wants to be an economist.   c) The Druze are a religious sect, who live mainly in the mountainous regions of Lebanon and southern Syria.   d) My uncle, who doesn't speak a word of English, told me that he is planning to visit America in the summer.   e) Yesterday I went to visit my grandmother, who is in hospital with a chest complaint.   f) Italians, who are well known for their love of music, have some of the world's greatest opera singers.

16. a) After walking for six miles in the hot sun, the man finally found a garage.   b) Before cooking the sardines, they washed them and cut them into pieces.   c) After landing in the sea and waiting for the rescue boats, the passengers finally escaped.   d) Before going on a boat trip, make sure that there is petrol in the spare can.

17. a) 'I'd like a single room,' he told the receptionist.   b) 'What's the time?' Carlos asked. 'Six o'clock,' I replied.   c) 'Follow the London road and turn left at the roundabout,' explained Tania.   d) 'It's very hot today,' said Boris. 'I think I'll go for a swim.'

18. *Suggested answer:*
    On Thursday Gabriella, who is a very close friend of mine, invited me to her house. She was having a small party for her daughter, Elena. My father, who doesn't work on Saturdays, offered to take me in his car and I arrived about two o'clock. The house, which was quite large, was full of people. There was a lot of noise from the children, who were playing with a plastic beach ball. Gabriella asked me if I wanted to meet Elena's teacher. I said 'Yes,' and so she took me into the garden and I was introduced to Koula, who was sitting under a tree. Gabriella brought us both some orange juice and cake, which she had baked for Elena's party. I want to be a teacher too, and so I asked Koula many questions about teaching. She told me that she had studied at a teacher's training college in Thessaloniki, which is a large city to the north-east of Athens. After leaving teacher training college, she went to teach in a small village school. Three years ago she moved to the city and started teaching at Elena's school, which is only half a kilometre from her home. I asked her what she liked most about teaching. 'The children,' she replied, 'they are lovely.' At that moment, the ball landed on the table and knocked the cake and orange juice onto the ground. 'Well, most of the time,' she added with a smile.

19. a) who   b) that   c) although   d) in order to   e) which   f) After   g) before   h) if   i) who   j) when

20. Paragraph A – e, c, b, f, d, a.
    Paragraph C – g, f, a, h, b, d, e, c.

25. One day last summer my family went for a **picnic** in a park near the sea. We **left** home early in the morning and found a quiet place under some trees. We put up the tent, which we always take with us, and my sister and I began to prepare some food. After eating, we **were** all resting near the **tent** and Somboon, **who** is my youngest son, was playing with a ball. I told him to go and **play** near the trees. A few minutes later he screamed and fell to the ground. We all ran over and found him holding his **foot**. 'What's the matter?' I **asked**. 'It's my foot,' he cried. 'Something bit me.' Then we **saw** a large snake in the grass. I told my husband to kill it quickly. He picked up a stick and

hit it hard until it was no longer moving. Then he said he would take **S**omboon to the hospital. We all went with him in the jeep. I was very **worried** because Somboon was breathing with difficulty.

26. 1) said,   2) explained,   3) told,   4) asked,
    5) added,   6) replied

27. worried: nervous, afraid, frightened, concerned, anxious, tense
    calm: relaxed, tranquil, confident, peaceful, quiet, still

28.

¹H	O	²R	I	³Z	O	N		⁴T	E	⁵A

(crossword grid)

```
 H O R I Z O N    ■ T E A
 A ■ U ■ N ■ ■    ■ R ■ L
 ⁶D O N E ■⁷E M ⁸P T Y ■ T
 ■ N ■ ■ ⁹T ■ ■ M ■ ■ ■ H
¹⁰A ■ E ■ H ■¹¹R ■ ■¹²W H O
¹³S C R E A M E D ■ A ■ U
 K ■ S ■ T ■ P ■¹⁴A S ■ G
 E ■ ¹⁵O ■¹⁶C L A P ■ ■ H
¹⁷D A R K ■ ■ I ■¹⁹P U²⁰T
 ■ I ■ ■ ■²¹F E E L ■ H
 ■²²C²³O U L D ■ ■²⁴Y E A R
²⁵W H E N ■ Y ■ ■ ■ ■ N
```

Unit Five

10. a) Rome – has – hotter summers – than – London.
    b) Fresh fruit juice – is – healthier – than – cola.
    c) Coconut palms – are usually – taller – than – date palms.   d) A boiled egg – is – easier to prepare – than – an omlette.

11. a) Chinese – is – more – difficult – to – learn – than – Farsi.   b) E-mail messages – are – less – personal – than – handwritten letters.   c) An ordinary phone – is – less – useful – than – a mobile phone.
    d) Gold – is – more – expensive – than – silver.

12. a) Victor is more intelligent then Ernesto.
    b) Watermelons are cheaper than pineapples.
    c) Istanbul is more beautiful than Ankara.
    d) Koshiba is better than Vanasonic.
    e) A mobile phone is quicker than rescue flares.

13. c) = defining   d) = non-defining

14. a) I managed to find the homework <u>which the teacher had asked me about</u>.
    b) On our trip to India last year the place <u>which I liked best</u> was Darjeeling.
    c) Yesterday in the supermarket I saw the woman <u>who reads the news on Channel 33</u>.
    d) That's the car <u>which I want to buy</u>.
    e) 'People <u>who need people</u> are the luckiest people in the world.'

15. a) That's the man who stole my bag.   b) We went to see that film that you recommended.   c) The car that I like the best is too expensive.   d) The waitress who we gave our order to has disappeared.   e) The country which has the largest population in the world is China.   f) Every year the college presents a prize to the student that gets the best results.

16. *Possible answers:*
    a) ... hit my car
    b) ... that I bought last week
    c) ... which I liked most on our trip last year
    d) ... who go to football matches

18. a) Canberra, which is the capital of Australia, is not the biggest city in the country.   b) The shop had sold out of Jasmine Mystery, which is my favourite perfume.   c) The man who robbed the bank was arrested yesterday.   d) The main course was sardines, which are popular in Portugal.
    e) Last week I wrote a letter to the college that I want to study in.   f) Yu Lin said she wanted to speak to the woman who was in charge of the shop.   g) The programme that I wanted to watch was cancelled at the last minute.   h) Peter, who is a well-known journalist, writes for a Cape Town newspaper.   i) All appointments have been cancelled by the president, who has a slight stomach upset.

19. a) On the one hand, b) But c) when d) less
    e) which f) However g) more h) who
    l) whereas j) Although

20. Paragraph 1) – e, b, c, d, f, a.
    Paragraph 2) – e, b, d, a, f, c.

21. a) the general reader b) formal/academic
    c) a friend (Aunt Sarah) d) informal/personal
    Letter: a) advertisement b) very interesting
    c) send me d) I am e) would like to find
    f) quite well g) a little h) a great deal i) very
    j) I have k) you wish l) I look forward to hearing from you m) Yours faithfully,

26. There are two buildings which (**they**) are **suitable** for the company. One is a building called Panorama House. It **is** located close to the city centre in Station Road. The total area is 1,350sq m. It has six floors and a small reception area. **There** are six toilets and a small kitchen. From the sixth floor there are **lovely** views of the city. The second possibility is a **building** called Park Mansions, which (**it**) is much larger **than** Panorama House. It has eight **floors**. The reception area is **bigger** too, **which** (**it**) is very important for the company. Unfortunately the rent is more **expensive** than the rent for Panorama House. It is $6,000 per month, **whereas** the rent for Panorama House is only $5,000. The location is less convenient too. Panorama House is (**more**) closer to the city centre.

27. *Suggested answer:*
There are **many** different types of plants, **for example** ferns, conifers and angiosperms. The largest group of plants are angiosperms, which **are also called** flowering plants. Flowering plants produce flowers which produce seeds and fruit. (**Well**,) Flowering plants **can be divided** into two more types. **These are called** monocots and dicots. The monocot, which means 'one seed-leaf' (**by the way**), has (**got**) long narrow leaves. The veins in the leaves are all **parallel**. An example of **a monocot** is the palm tree. On the other hand, the dicot (**i.e.** 'two seed-leaf') has (**got**) broader leaves. The veins are **also** different. There **is** a main vein and (**then**) there are **smaller** veins branching off. A tomato plant is an example of a dicot. These two kinds of angiosperm **can be seen** in the **diagram**.

28. hot – hotter – the hottest; big – bigger – the biggest; wet – wetter – the wettest; nice – nicer – the nicest; heavy – heavier – the heaviest; dry – drier – the driest; easy – easier – the easiest

29. good – better – the best; bad – worse – the worst; much/many – more – the most; little – less – the least; old – older– the oldest

30. a) Baikal – deepest   b) longest – Nile
c) Indonesia – greatest (largest)   d) highest – Venezuela   e) coldest – Antarctica
f) Al Azziziyah – hottest

31. a) suitable   b) comfortable   c) pleasant
d) personal   e) interesting   f) difficult   g) reliable
h) exciting   i) intelligent

Vertical word = important.

Unit Six

1.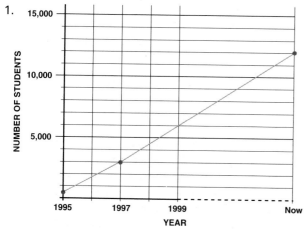

4. a) 1 – mainframe computer   2 – silicon chip
3 – the desktop PC

For the last fifty years computers have been getting smaller, cheaper and more powerful.

5. a) they = computers; one = a computer; this = the invention of the silicon chip; then = 1981
b) millions of calculations; the first computer which was able to store a program; sales of computers

6.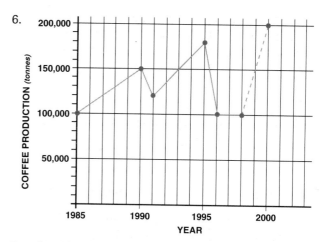

7. a) 3 b) 3 c) 1 d) 3 e) 2 f) 1

8. a) Felix – has been working – in a bank – since 1999.
b) The boys – have been washing – their car – since six o'clock.   c) I – have known – Sarah – since she was a little girl.   d) My family – have kept – horses – for many years.   e) Andy – has been waiting for – a bus – for twenty minutes.   f) People – have grown – rice in the valley – for centuries.

11. 1) There are two possible ways of joining each sentence, as shown in a).

1) Keiko is studying business studies, English and computing because she wants to work for a large multinational company. OR Because she wants to work for a large multinational company, Keiko is studying business studies, English and computing.
2) Coffee production fell dramatically last year because many trees were destroyed by bad weather.
3) More and more people are buying computers because they are becoming cheaper and cheaper.
4) Nina couldn't come to the birthday party yesterday because she was taking an examination at the college.
5) The government is building ten new schools because the population of the country has been increasing rapidly in recent years.
6) Boris has been trying to save money for the last six months because he wants to go on holiday to San Francisco in the summer.

14. 1) When the college opened, there were only 500 students and three faculties.
2) As the machine spins around, the juice is extracted from the fruit.
3) In order to increase coffee production, many new trees had to be planted.
4) If you have got a mobile phone, you can make a phone call from anywhere.
5) Although the weather was bad, we decided to make the trip to Star Island.
6) Because the weather was bad, we decided to cancel the trip to Star Island.

15. *Possible answers:*
a) is from Canada,
b) are located just outside Cairo,
c) was president of South Africa,

d) is studying at a university in Washington.

e) is a beautiful old city in Turkey.

f) is a popular dish in the Arab world,

16. a) The first computer able to store a program was built at Manchester University in 1948. b) The man wearing a brown jacket is a chemistry professor. c) The tall tower built like a rocket is the Holiday Hotel. d) The president is the short, fat man speaking to the old lady. e) The country most famous for growing coffee is Brazil. f) Andrea Borcelli is a blind Italian singer known for his wonderful voice.

17. **A**eroplanes have been getting bigger and faster over the years. **T**he first modern aeroplane was the **B**oeing 247, which was introduced in 1933. **I**t had room for 10 passengers. **D**uring the **S**econd **W**orld **W**ar the jet engine was developed. **T**he first jet airliner, which was called the **C**omet, started service in 1952. **I**t had four jet engines and could fly at 885kph. **L**ater, in 1958, **P**an **A**merican **A**irlines introduced the Boeing 707, which could carry 112 passengers. **B**ecause of the powerful engines, the plane was able to cross the **A**tlantic from **N**ew **Y**ork to **L**ondon in less than eight hours, which was half the time of the old propeller aircraft.

18. a) *Possible answer:*

Dear Elena,

I'm writing this letter to you from my bed. I broke my leg badly three weeks ago on the stairs in the college. I was in a hurry <u>because I was late for class. As I was running down the stairs from the first floor to the ground floor</u>, I slipped and fell to the bottom. I felt a terrible pain in my left leg and I couldn't move. At the hospital the doctor, <u>who is a friend of my father's</u>, told me that my leg was broken. After resetting my leg in plaster, he said that I should rest at home for at least a month and then come back to see him. He told me to phone him <u>if I needed help</u>. Since then I've been at home, <u>which has been rather boring</u>. I've been getting better bit by bit. I've been reading books and magazines and watching TV, but I can't wait until I can walk again. Sometimes I sit in the garden, <u>which is just outside my bedroom window</u>, if it's not too hot. My older sister, <u>who's not working at the moment</u>, has been looking after me. She's been wonderful!

Please write and let me know your news!

Best wishes,

Sarah

b) informal/personal style

19. d – i – e – c – f – g – a – h – b

20. a) but   b) Because of this   c) However   d) which
e) also   f) Since   g) Whereas   h) which
i) Because   j) Although

25. a) Global warming is caused by an **increase** in the amount of carbon dioxide in the Earth's atmosphere. Carbon dioxide **is** produced naturally by vegetation.

It is **an** important part of the atmosphere. It traps the sun's heat. It warms the surface of the Earth. Normally there is a balance between the gases in the **atmosphere**. In recent years the amount of carbon dioxide has **gone** up. This is **because** of the burning of fossil fuels and the destruction of forests. The temperature of the Earth's surface **has** been going up. **This** has meant changes in **the** Earth's climate. Many parts of the world are becoming **hotter** and drier. Other parts are experiencing more storms and rainfall. Sea level (**it**) has also been **rising**. This is because the polar ice-caps have been melting.

b) *Suggested improvement:*

Global warming is caused by an increase in the amount of carbon dioxide in the Earth's atmosphere. Carbon dioxide, which is produced naturally by vegetation, is an important part of the atmosphere. It traps the sun's heat and as a result warms the surface of the Earth. Normally there is a balance between the gases in the atmosphere. In recent years, however, the amount of carbon dioxide has gone up because of the burning of fossil fuels and the destruction of forests. As a result the temperature of the Earth's surface has been going up, which has meant changes in the Earth's climate. Many parts of the world are becoming hotter and drier, while other parts are experiencing more storms and rainfall. Sea level has also been rising. This is because the polar ice-caps have been melting.

26. increase: go up, grow, improve, rise
decrease: go down, fall, collapse, drop

27. a) Chemistry   b) Physics   c) Biology
d) History   e) Geography   f) Mathematics
g) Computer Science

28. a) Science   b) Law   c) Education   d) Arts
e) Engineering

29.

¹G	E	T	²T	I	N	G			³I		⁴S	
O			H					⁵U	N	⁶T	I	L
⁷N	⁸O	W	A	¹⁰D	A	Y	S			¹¹O	N	
¹²E	X	I	T		L		E				C	
	T			T			¹³D	R	¹⁴I	E	¹⁵D	
	¹⁶W	H	¹⁷I	C	H				N		R	
	H		T		O	R			C		O	
	E			U			¹⁹F	O	R		P	
²⁰T	R	Y	²¹I	N	G		E		E		P	
	E		T		H		L		²²A	²³R	E	
	²⁴A	L	S	²⁵O		²⁶C	L	O	²⁷S	E	D	
²⁸A	S			²⁹N	O			³⁰F	E	D		